San Francisco Theatre Research

Vol. 2

MONOGRAPHS

III: TOM MAGUIRE
IV: DR. DAVID G. (YANKEE) ROBINSON
V: M. B. LEAVITT

WILDSIDE PRESS

Lawrence Estavan, Editor.   San Francisco, June 1938
Monographs III, IV and V from Theatre Research
W.P.A. Project 8386, O.P. 465-03-3-286

TABLE OF CONTENTS

TOM MAGUIRE -- (1820?-1896)

	PAGES
The Napoleon of Impresarios	1-69
The First Napoleonic Decade (1850-1860)	1-12
The Man and the Times	1
The Glass of Fashion	1
Tom's Genesis	2
First Western Appearance	3
His Knack for Ballyhoo	4
Jenny Lind and the Jinx	5
The Third Jenny Lind	6
More Trouble with Jenny	7
Tom Sells a City Hall	8
Imports Biscaccianti	9
Bull Fights and Steamer Day	9
A Steamer Day Calamity	10
The Monopolist	11
Complaints About Tom	12
Monarch of All He Surveys	13-24
Minstrels and Minstrelsy	13
Spectacles and Sensation Dramas	15
The Devil in San Francisco	16
Scouting in the East	17
Stage Attractions	18
The Wholesale Importer	19
"Jack Pudding" Courtaine	20
Courtaine's Fortune	21
Other Notable Imports	22
His Love for Grand Opera	24-33
Maguire's Op'ry House	26
His First Imported Outfit	26
Getting His Fill	27
More Grief with the Bianchis	29
Disastrous Losses	30
Interlude in Paris	31
Opera Continued	32

TABLE OF CONTENTS (cont.)

PAGES

Battles With the Law..34-42

    Scandal Sheets... 34
    Critics Sued for Slander................................. 35
    Benefit for Thomas Maguire............................... 36
    "A Disorderly House"..................................... 37
    "Maguire's Japs"... 37
    The Black Crook.. 38
    Burlesque on Plagiarists................................. 39
    Mrs. Grundy in Court..................................... 39
    Vestvali: the Magnificent................................ 40
    Pirate Brought to Bay.................................... 41

The Decline of Tom Maguire..43-52

    Maguire on Hamlet.. 43
    Benefit and Testimonials................................. 44
    Letter of Appreciation................................... 45
    Another Preliminary Announcement......................... 47
    A Review of the Benefit.................................. 48
    "A Real Genuine Original Pioneer"........................ 49
    Tom: A Man of Experience................................. 50
    Departure for the East................................... 51
    Footlight Flash.. 52
    Drumming Up Another Benefit.............................. 52

His Waterloo..53-59

    The Passion Play... 53
    Reaping a Whirlwind...................................... 54
    Temptation and Penalty................................... 55
    Partners and Pretenders.................................. 56
    Desperate Stunts... 57
    A Deal with Lucky Baldwin................................ 57
    The Handwriting on the Wall.............................. 59
    The Shut-down of Baldwin's............................... 59

Exile in the East...60-69

    New Expectations... 60
    Alms for Oblivion.. 61
    On the Death of Tom Maguire.............................. 62
    The Dead Napoleon; A Final Accounting.................... 63
    Parting Words; Final Evaluation.......................... 67
    Tom Maguire's Career..................................... 69

TABLE OF CONTENTS (Cont.)

DR. DAVID G. (YANKEE) ROBINSON

	PAGES
THE PIONEER OF DRAMA IN SAN FRANCISCO	72-108

Early Years	73
Advent into San Francisco	73
The Dramatic Museum	74
Premiere Performance	75
Favorite Songs	76
Repertoire and Cast	78
Benefit Performance	80
Siege of Cholera	81
Dramatic Museum's Busy Period	83
Novelty Presentations	84
Company Criticized	85
Robinson as Politician	86
A New Theatre	88
New Building Erected	89
Theatrical Competition	91
American Theatre Opens	91
Robinson-Stark Feud	93
Telegraph Hill Home	95
Robinson-Maguire Reconciliation	96
Coming of Lola Montez	98
Original Lola Burlesque	99
Manages Sue Robinson	101
Lotta-Sue Rivalry	102
New and Original Burlesque	103
Career Abruptly Ended	104
Leaves Vivid Memories	105
Representative Parts	107
Theatres Associated with Doctor Robinson	107
Bibliography of Dr. Robinson's Works	107
Bibliography	108

TABLE OF CONTENTS (Cont.)

MICHAEL M. LEAVITT -- (1843 - 1935)

	PAGES
Actor-Manager and Father of Vaudeville	109-142
Genesis of Vaudeville	110
Moppet Impresario and Actor	112
A Start in Earnest	113
Branching out -- on Tour	116
A Series of Adventures	119
En Route to the West	123
Variety, Burlesque and Vaudeville	125
Established in San Francisco	127
Success and Affluence	130
Retires from San Francisco after 20 years	136
Some of his Business Associates	140
Booking Managers who Worked for Leavitt	140
Performers and Companies Managed by Leavitt	141-143
Theatres Managed or Leased by Leavitt	143
Press Agents who Worked for Leavitt	144
Bibliography	145
Newspapers and Periodicals	145

THOMAS MAGUIRE
1820 - 1896

PHOTO COURTESY M. H. de YOUNG MUSEUM

TOM MAGUIRE

The First Napoleonic Decade (1850-1860)
The Man And The Times

Tom Maguire who rose from cab driver to gambler, from gambler to saloon keeper, and from saloon keeper to become one of the country's great impresarios has often been called the Napoleon of San Francisco's theatrical world. But this is an easy analogy. True, like Napoleon he thirsted for power, plotted great campaigns, schemed ruthlessly and maneuvered with success. Like Napoleon, after many victories, he failed and went into exile. For nearly three decades he dominated his chosen sphere; his career was bound up with perhaps the city's most turbulent and picturesque period. But he was an illiterate back-stage Napoleon, a self-made man with all the apparent pride and self-assertion of such a one. He was shrewd, opportunistic, and full of grandiose illusions. He had an instinct for the theatrical and an intuitive knowledge of what would draw a crowd. He furnished a pleasure-hungry city with the spectacles it wanted.

THE GLASS OF FASHION

Considered one of the handsomest men in San Francisco, Maguire at the height of his glory was a familiar sight about town. Every morning about 11 o'clock he would appear in Washington Street holding his levees on the curbstone in front of his theatre. He was fashionably dressed, with an enormous diamond in his scarf, a solitaire on his finger, a heavy gold watch chain hanging from his waistcoat. Suave and well groomed, Maguire was a typical California gambler type.

GENESIS

His beginnings and earlier career have yielded little to the scrutiny of the biographer, and what is known of his pre-Napoleonic days is due chiefly to Dame Rumor and Master Hear-say. There is one source, however, in the person of James O'Meara, an old California journalist, whose reminiscences on Tom's early life give a vivid impression of reality and of one side of his character. On Jan. 25, 1896, he sent The Bulletin the following memoranda on Tom's beginnings. They illustrate the reckless nature of the man at that time, and the desperate courage that marked him then as well as in his later San Francisco career:

> "I first met Maguire in New York in 1846. He was driver of a carriage hack, with a stand in Park Row, near the old Park Theatre, between it and the Lovejoy Hotel. Tom was dressed roughly in hackman style; wore an overcoat made from a long, blue blanket, with the deep, dark-blue striped band, two inches wide, running around the bottom of the skirt. I got him to vote at a primary election of Democrats on Fulton Street, to nominate Alderman J.C. Stoneall of the Second Ward.
>
> "A few months later I witnessed a rough-and-tumble fight between Maguire and Dick Donnell-- a flashy rowdy of the Tapis Franc, No. 10 Ann Street, in the lobby of the Park Theatre, the

winner to be 'the man' of Little Em the bright but not pretty Becky Sharp of her coterie. Maguire won. Afterwards he married her, I believe, and she was the Mrs. Tom Maguire of his subsequent California Jenny Lind Theatre and Broderick periods.

"In the winter of 1846-47 Maguire was a partner of Bill Drayton -- a handsome, dressy, smooth and accomplished New York 'tom boy' -- and they kept the bars of the second and third tiers of the Park Theatre. In 1847 Maguire and Captain Isaiah Rynders, Chieftain of Tammany, and leader of the noted Empire Club, were partners in a famous saloon at the head of City Hall Place.

"I next saw Tom in San Francisco. He arrived, I think, early in 1850, and he and Ned Gallagher kept a large frame saloon on the site of the Jenny Lind Theatre, which Maguire built. In the saloon, late one night, while Rube Withers, son of Withers, President of the New York Bank on Wall Street, was in the city prison awaiting trial for murder, I saw Tom Maguire stand off Bob Edwards, a young Philadelphia desperado, who had killed several men. Edwards stood with his six-shooter pointed at Maguire, who showed no fear, until a policeman came in and arrested Edwards for killing a Mexican out at the Mission.

"In 1853 Maguire faced Vi Turner, a desperate sport, and bitterly cursed him on the corner of Washington and Montgomery Streets. There was no back-down in Tom Maguire.

"By the way, at his request, I was at the funeral of Tom's father, in 1850, who was buried at North Beach from a small frame building, then St. Francis Catholic Church, on the site of the present edifice.

"During the lifetime of David C. Broderick in San Francisco Tom Maguire's was his home and he was on most confidential terms with Tom and his wife -- the Little Em of New York times."

FIRST WESTERN APPEARANCE

Maguire came to San Francisco with thousands of

fortune hunters during the delirious gold rush days. He continued his activities as saloon and hotel keeper and gambler while he sponsored various types of theatrical ventures. Arriving in September 1849, he soon afterwards became proprietor of the Parker House. Tom fitted up his first theatre above the saloon of this establishment and called it the Jenny Lind. The nearness of the saloon was a source of small regret to Tom and his patrons. Most of the early theatres boasted of bars adjoining their lobbies. A little later Maguire was to operate a gambling hall and saloon, picturesquely named The Snug, for the convenience of his Opera House patrons.

HIS KNACK FOR BALLYHOO

Maguire was a keen judge of character and was seldom mistaken in offering what the public would buy in the way of entertainment. He never spared expense in engaging the most competent directors, managers, and technicians. The most famous stars of the day appeared in his theatres. He built his houses to suit the needs of a growing community; they were the most lavishly appointed and magnificent in town. His task was not easy in these early times of violence and unrest. He rose and fell on successive waves of prosperity and depression; he kept himself going with a gambler's wit and an unusual knack for showmanship.

In the following pages we shall trace his progress from his arrival in San Francisco and his subsequent arrogation of theatrical power, through his Napoleonic days, his era of see-sawing fortunes, his decade of decline, and finally his end in want and destitution.

JENNY LIND AND THE JINX

Maguire's first theatre of any pretensions was built above his gambling saloon, the Parker House, in 1850. It was christened Jenny Lind in honor of the famous singer of the day who, contrary to popular opinion, never sang in San Francisco. Maguire engaged James Stark as director, and productions of classics such as Macbeth, Hamlet, King Lear, Much Ado About Nothing, Richelieu, Pizarro, The Rivals, and many English comedies were given with great success and profit.

The first Jenny Lind was destroyed early in May, 1851, in a disastrous fire which swept San Francisco. Maguire immediately rebuilt it. Nine days after its second opening, on June 22, it was burnt to the ground in another great fire, the sixth in a series. Maguire was having hard luck.

Sympathetic to his losses, the Herald on June 26, 1851, reports the calamity in the following terms:

> "One of the hardest cases connected with the fire was the destruction of the Jenny Lind Theatre, just erected and elegantly fitted up by Mr. Thomas Maguire. He had been burnt out in every fire that has occurred in the city and now again before he has removed the scaffolding from his building it is laid low in ashes. The fire seems to have a special spite against him. It appeared to pick him out from others, his being the only building in the block that was burnt. He is going to try it once more we understand. He intends erecting a large brick theatre, one story high at first, the walls of

which have already been raised some five or six feet. The Bella Union, Verandah, Custom House, El Dorado, and California Exchange have again escaped almost unscorched..."

THE THIRD JENNY LIND

Undaunted, Maguire built a third Jenny Lind Theatre, this time of stone, and his most magnificent building to date. The facade was of finely dressed yellow-tinted sandstone brought from Australia. A finished piece of workmanship, the prevailing color of the interior was a light pink "which was rendered brilliant and graceful by gilding tastefully applied." The chief feature of the back-drop was a romantic ruin. Richly carved and decorated proscenium boxes added much to the splendor of the auditorium.

Seating two thousand and proudly claiming to be the equal of any theatre in America, the new Jenny Lind opened on October 4, 1851, with a fine cast presenting, <u>All That Glitters Is Not Gold</u>. Maguire was established as a worthy citizen. On the occasion of a benefit for the proprietor in December of the same year, the <u>Alta California</u> commented:

"MR. MAGUIRE'S BENEFIT. The walls of the Jenny Lind must be made to reverberate the echoes of honest and timely applause to-night, in token of a heartfelt welcome to a worthy beneficiare, the founder of this magnificent temple of the drama, Mr. Thomas Maguire--On the very spot where now stands the noblest and most imposing edifice in the state, where now flourishes a theatre which for interior beauty, grandeur and comfort shall compare with the best in America, Mr. Maguire has four times witnessed his enterprise crumble in ashes, and his fortune 'dissolve into thin air.' Surely this community owes Mr. Maguire a deep debt of gratitude for the display of energy which, after a long series of endurance and disappointment, has at length established in our midst one of the most permanent sources of good, one of the best correctives of society, and most efficient instruments of moral reform ever instituted in our city."

MORE TROUBLE

But trouble was in store in spite of these encouraging sentiments. The fine prospects with which the third Jenny Lind opened were not realized during the following months. The overhead, the upkeep of the numerous small gold town theatres of which Maguire had been acquiring control, the premature branching out into that monopoly of theatrical business which he was to establish successfully later on, proved Maguire's undoing. He had too many irons in the fire.

Still putting up a fine front in February, Maguire succumbed to the current financial depression by the end of June, though before this he had played an occasional trump card at the Jenny Lind. One of these was the introduction locally of Wilmarth Waller, young American tragedian, who played "heavy" roles for about a week. Caroline Chapman, establishing herself as a local favorite, drew fairly good houses in May. The mechanics were impatient, however, and the builders besieged Maguire demanding payment for services rendered in erecting the magnificent Jenny Lind. Our manager tried to negotiate, but without success. Cash was demanded, and there was no cash.

TOM SELLS A CITY HALL

In desperation Maguire hit upon a brilliant scheme. He would sell the Jenny Lind to the city for use as a city hall. This would mean a substantial sum in his pocket and would re-establish his credit. He promptly entered into negotiations with the city fathers. Swearing that it was several thousands below cost, Maguire asked for the Jenny Lind the sum of $200,000. Much discussion, debating and bitter feeling were aroused by the proposition. The whole city seemed agitated. For months the matter was an important topic of conversation. At an open meeting on the Plaza on June 2, vehement oratory tried to influence public opinion. A certain Dr. Gihon, one of the authors of The Annals, protested with strong feeling, according to the Herald:

> "I will acknowledge that it is a splendid building -- a beautiful building -- a beautiful theatre, but for God's sake let it be kept as a theatre, (laughter) and let us not allow the Board of Aldermen to put their hands in the public treasury, for the sum of two hundred thousand dollars, and make us buy it against our will...It would seem as if they regard the public treasury as a goose, to be plucked by them at their leisure."

Mr. David C. Broderick spoke in favor of the purchase, but was shouted down. The meeting then separated peaceably, to the surprise of many, as a collision was expected. The matter was a very important topic in San Francisco for many months. After the actual purchase certain citizens sought to obtain an injunction against the Board of Aldermen, and there was a great deal of complaint about necessary remodeling. The deed was done, however, and the city fathers moved to their new address.

IMPORTS BISCACCIANTI

His credit good again, Maguire proceeded to build another theatre, a new "Temple of the Muses" -- less gorgeous perhaps but more practical. San Francisco Hall was its name for the time being. Opened by Signora Elisa Biscaccianti, it was "consecrated to Thespis" on December 25, 1852. Young Junius Booth was installed as manager. A week after the opening, Maguire's foremost managerial rival, Doc Robinson, who had served a jovial term as Alderman, was engaged to play in the theatre. San Francisco's two Little Giants resumed professional relations.*

Fresh from recent triumphs in the States and in Europe, petite, lustrous-eyed, and in the prime of her beauty, Elisa Biscaccianti, the new offering of Tom Maguire, was the first star of any eminence to come to San Francisco. She dared to venture in an unknown musical field which P. T. Barnum feared to risk with his Swedish Nightingale, Jenny Lind, and which the Swan of Erin, Kate Hayes, dared not hazard. As soon as she had demonstrated that big money was to be made in this distant frontier town by the best of art, San Francisco leaped into world fame as "the actor's El Dorado."

BULL FIGHTS AND STEAMER DAY

Besides the theatre, citizens patronized other and

---
*See monograph on Doc Robinson, in this volume. Note about the previous feud.

sometimes more elementary forms of entertainment. There were still bull fights occasionally in 1859; freak shows and circuses still drew the crowds. There were always horse races, balls, May festivals at Russ Gardens or some other picnic spot. Panoramas of historic or geographic interest, concerts, lectures, Sunday camp-meetings attracted a good part of the pleasure-seeking public. In 1857 walking marathons were also popular.

Distinct from the legitimate theatre which usually put on classics and pieces expressing lofty sentiment, there were many other less elevated types of entertainment. Beside the numerous amateur shows and the foreign-language productions, there was the variety entertainment of a cabaret type which came to flower on the Barbary Coast. Of variety halls the best known is perhaps the famous Bella Union.

A STEAMER DAY CALAMITY

In spite of the development of the theatre and its popularity in the gold rush towns, the western population, on the whole was simple in its make-up. Steamer Day in San Francisco at this time was still a cause of the greatest excitement. It was calamity for a show or a star to open on the day when a steamer was scheduled to reach port. When Tom Maguire sometimes forgot this, his Opera House suffered. Neville's <u>The Fantastic City</u> tells of an instance:

> "It was the opening night of Tom's season, a brilliant much-heralded premiere of a Shakespearean star in his finest role. The audience

was a 'galaxy of fashion,' in the time-honored phrase of local drama critics, but attention was divided. The established signal for arrival of a steamer at night was a shot from lookout on Telegraph Hill, and the audience strained its ears not so much to catch the well-remembered lines as the signal from the watch tower. In the middle of the fifth act it came. Without hesitation the audience rose in a body. Men grabbed their hats and rushed forth, women followed, hurriedly donning their cloaks, while the actors stared in amazement and chagrin and the more experienced stage hands unceremoniously rang down the curtain on the emptying house."

But later, when steamboats became less extraordinary, it was the colored minstrels, the Japanese tumblers, and the great Professor Belew, tamer of wild horses, who proved to be the stronger attraction.

THE MONOPOLIST

Fortune is fickle -- there were booms and depressions -- and Tom had his ups and downs. For a while it seemed as if the rip-snorting days of the theatre had passed. Times were dull in San Francisco. Again and again we read of the scarcity of money, the unpredictable caprice of audiences, the lack of amusement attractions.

Maguire had adopted a regular routine. Stars appearing in San Francisco were routed through the interior to play at small theatres in mining towns. There was a system of commuting from California to Australia. Nevertheless, the important events were the appearance of stars drawn by curiosity, clever managers, or advantageous contracts, to visit a remote El Dorado which could be reached only through the

Isthmus of Panama or around the Horn by dint of much discomfort and lost time. The result of this system was that San Francisco periodically had cause to complain of either a "dearth" or a "plethora" of theatrical stars.

COMPLAINTS ABOUT TOM

It was at this period that a stranded actor in San Francisco wrote to a colleague in New York:

> "The conditions in which theatricals now are is truly deplorable; there are two theatres in San Francisco, one each in Sacramento, Stockton, Sonoma, and Marysville -- all of which it is understood are under one management, which exercises a kind of despotism over the profession, and compels actors to come to their terms.. Living is so high, unless the pay is enormous, an actor cannot save a dollar, and the amount required to come home so great, that he must either play for a mere living, or go to the mines and die..."

Tom Maguire was gradually approaching the peak of his power and influence in the California theatre. Not only did he control a successful theatre in San Francisco, but he had leases or agreements with managers or owners of many small theatres in the interior.

Indeed, in February 1858, the Sacramento Bee complained that Tom, having leases of both the Sacramento and the Forrest Theatres, at that time controlled all the best stock players and most of the prominent theatres in the state and "may be said to have a complete monopoly of theatricals in California." At any rate, in the last years of the Gold Rush Decade it was Maguire who constantly fed the flame of the theatre with new material from the East. He himself took passage to the Atlantic states in May 1857, and later had an agent in the East as well as a scout in Australia working for him.

MONARCH OF ALL HE SURVEYS

Dramatis Personae: Jawbone, A Yank.

It was during the turbulent sixties -- while the Civil War was raging in the South and Lincoln, the man of the people, governed a divided nation, and the first transcontinental railroad was under construction, uniting east and west -- that Tom Maguire came to full bloom as the Napoleon of Theatre Managers in California. His strongest rival, Doc Robinson, had journeyed East in search of a "nobler and higher career in the theatre" and reached the land of his fathers, dying of fever in Alabama. He was soon forgotten.

San Francisco was leaving its embryo existence. Its population of talent and education ceased their menial occupations, emerged from their filthy lodgings and doffed their coarse red shirts for Chesterfieldian apparel. All their wants now had to be of the same luxuriant kind. The circuses no longer drew the crowds.

MINSTRELS

Maguire undertook to supply the changing tastes of a restless public by building in 1859 the Eureka Minstrel Hall, a variety theatre. Opera and minstrel shows were popular at this time; dramatic pieces and actors and actresses were on the decline. Maguire himself was strongly attracted to minstrel shows and developed this kind of entertainment to new heights. The programs were often original, rich in humor.

His Minstrel Hall opened with the afterwards famous and unrivaled San Francisco Minstrels, headed by Birch, Backus, and Bernard, and later strengthened by David Wambold. According to Clay Greene's Memoirs, Billy Birch and Charley Backus have never been excelled as end men of the oldest and best class of minstrelsy. While Bernard was a great baritone, Wambold had as glorious a tenor voice as ever sang in a minstrel first part, Greene says, adding:

> "Their success was so prodigious at Maguire's that this notable quartet of entertainers decided to go into business on their own account, proceeded to New York and, under the name of Birch, Wambold, Bernard & Backus (sub-titled the San Francisco Minstrels), played with continuous success for many years."

During the late summer and early fall of 1862 Maguire undoubtedly had things much his own way.* For much of the time his was the only legitimate theatre open in the city. On August 9, Maguire advertised a new Boucicault play, Jeanie Deans, otherwise known as The Heart of Midlothian. On August 13 he added Jean Davenport to his fine cast and turned to the classics, after what the papers termed as "unparalleled success" of the Boucicault plays. On August 28, the Grand Italian and English Opera Company, still under the direction of S. Lyster, replaced the dramatic cast for three weeks.

---

* The following paragraphs, to page 18, are taken from Annals of The San Francisco Stage, (Federal Theatre, unpub. Mss.)

SPECTACLES

When spectacles and sensation dramas became all the rage, Maguire naturally responded to the new public interest. On March 30, 1863, he presented the elaborate spectacle, The Enchanted Beauty. After a run of ten days, the possibilities of this type of production so impressed Maguire that he continued to interlard his plays with ballets, adding Mlle. Caroline Acosta and M. Hippolyte Wiethoff to his company at the end of the month and recruiting for them a corps de ballet of some fifty local women. On May 5 Maguire showed, for the first time in California, Blondette, or The Naughty Prince and Pretty Peasant, another romantic spectacle.

On July 30 the American opened with a New Local Sensation Drama, entitled The Devil in San Francisco, based on the opera of Don Giovanni. The play was "one of the most successful local burlesques ever introduced on the California stage." In the cast, as advertised, were:

Don Giovanni, A devil among the women
    with songs..... Mrs. Julia Thoman

Chinawoman, Ah You, a feature of San Francisco
    and of the play..... Nellie Brown

Proserpine, afterwards a female Cheap John, with her famous
    song, "The Female Auctioneer"
    Miss Jennie Mandeville

Spitfire, afterwards a San Francisco newsboy with songs.......
    Miss Alicia Mandeville

Mrs. Fifer, of the codfish aristocracy
    Miss Howard

Sulphurina, Head Devil......... Mr. A.R. Phelps

Cheapy, prize baby, for exhibition at the
    State Agricultural Fair at
        Sacramento............... Mr. Ryer

Jawbone, A "Yank," comical......... Mr. Thoman

Toward the end of the month Maguire added another "novelty," a Professor Bushnell, who performed electro-biological feats as an entr'acte specialty. But the spectacle play was not to be Maguire's most important contribution to the local theatre in 1863. On May 16 he offered Lucille Western's version of a famous play, East Lynne. The critics were not enthusiastic about what the Bulletin reviewer called "the latest contribution to the sensational school of the drama," but the Bulletin writer admitted its effectiveness. In the Bulletin of May 17, 1863, we read:

> "The novel is a very painful one, but in the drama it is still more so. The morality and taste of such pieces is doubtful, yet people will see them and sit them out."

SENSATION DRAMAS

Maguire continued to capitalize on this new vogue. Says the Bulletin of June 2, 1863:

> "Sensation drama bears away here. Following East Lynne and The Dead Heart, we are tonight to have The Mistake of Life. This piece has not yet been performed in this country. Mr. Mayo and Mr. Thorne have been happily contrasted in some recent pieces; the one representing the romantic, brave, virtuous, proud young man, overwhelmed by misfortune and the other polished, unscrupulous rascal, triumphant for a time, but in the end fated to bite the dust. The heroine, represented by Mrs. Edwin, is of course the female counterpart of Mr. Mayo's role. Mr. Barry is the funny man, par excellence, of the piece--neither very virtuous nor wicked."

By way of variation, during June 1863, Maguire offered Mrs. Hayne and J. H. Taylor in a "Grand Combination" of old-timers, following with two patriotic war dramas as July 4 turned to national affairs. On July 20 he once more reverted to conservative drama, presenting Annette Ince in classic and heroic spectacle roles with one exception: this was her performance of the dual role of Lady Isabel and Mme. Vine in East Lynne -- parts played earlier by Sophie Edwin and Mrs. Hayne.

After a very discouraging autumn Maguire made a magnificent recovery during late November. On the 16th, Charles Wheatleigh opened at the Opera House in Boucicault's After Dark, a Tale of London Life, rights for which Maguire had purchased in the East through the good offices of D. C. Anderson, recently sojourning in London. Said the Figaro and Dramatic Review on November 16, 1863:

> "An audience such as has not gladdened the hearts of the Opera House management in many weeks assembled to do honor to this latest melodrama. The play ran through December 3, on which night the Alhambra opened a new burlesque, After Dark Brought to Light."

SCOUTING IN THE EAST

Maguire, leaving his Academy and Opera House in other hands, departed on February 1869, to seek new talent and "novelties" in the East. His theatres offered varied bills, vacillating from Japanese gymnasts (the city was suffering from a Flying Trapeze craze) and Martin the Wizard, to

Shakespeare. During the spring his Opera House presented in succession: Lady Don, Jennie Parker, John McCullough, Alice Kingsbury, Sophie Edwin, Amy Stone. Plays ranged from "sensation" pieces to ineffective local creations bitterly criticized by the newspapers.

STAGE ATTRACTIONS

Tom's theatres during his managership were generally houses of real entertainment. His one-time call boy, Johnny Ryan, has listed a few of the attractions he had seen. Said Johnny Ryan to Pauline Jacobson who interviewed him for the Bulletin Aug. 18, 1917:

> "My job didn't last long it seems, but while it did, I appreciated fully my chance to enjoy it; and such a chance now comes to few. In those days I saw:

Edwin Forrest	in Coriolanus; Virginius; first app. at Maguire's May 14, 1866 in Brutus.
Charles Kean	as Cardinal Woolsey and Louis XI
Boucicault	in Hamlet
Charles Wheatleigh	in The Octoroon
Daniel Bandmann	in Narcisse (opened at Maguire's Oct. 2, 1865)
Menken	in Mazeppa
Signor Enrico Bianchi	in Macbeth
Edwin Booth	as Iago
Alice Kingsbury	as Fanchon
Alice Dunning	in Frou Frou
Mrs. F. M. Bates	as Cleopatra
Charles R. Thorne	as Marc Anthony
J. B. Booth	in Othello
Sophie Edwin	in East Lynne
Ristori	as Elizabeth
McKean	in The Robbers
Harry Perry	in Monte Cristo
Lawrence Barrett	in Rosedale
Lady Don	in Kenilworth (1st. App. Aug. 6, 1866 at Maguire's; closed on Sept. 22)

Mrs. D. P. Bowers	as Lady Macbeth
Lucille Western	in The French Spy
Frank Lawlor	in Enoch Arden
Joe Jefferson	in Rip Van Winkle
Jim Herne	in Marble Hearts
Jeffreys Lewis	in Diplomacy
Mrs. Judah	in Romeo and Juliet
Mrs. C. R. Saunders	in The Two Orphans
Dan Setchell	in Dombey and Son
Frank Mayo	in The Romance of a Poor Man
Harry Courtaine	in Irish Comedy
Januschek	in her German portrayals
Modjeska	in her matchless plays

"And every one of these, and many other actors of merit, were supported by a stock company of high-class actors who played their parts with intelligence, and played them well."

THE WHOLESALE IMPORTER

During this period, no actor was too great nor his salary too high to keep him off the boards of Maguire's theatre. He brought out here at great cost by way of the Isthmus and across the plains the greatest actors, the great show pieces, dramas, minstrels, and operas. Nearly every play Shakespeare ever wrote was produced at his theatre. In all there are said to have been twenty interpretations of Hamlet.

Not only did he build up a matchless minstrel company, but also a dramatic stock company that won the recognition of the world: John McCullough, tragedian; Mrs. Saunders; Mrs. Judah, a great "bit" actress; Charles Thorne, great society villain; Frank Mayo; Billy Barry, great low comedian;

Lucy Sweet; Mrs. Bowers; Sophie Edwin, who played East Lynne; J. B. Booth, Jr., and David Anderson, great in old men's parts.

Frank Mayo had been employed in various minor capacities at Maguire's Opera House (peddling peanuts, captain of the supers, and the like) when he became stage struck. He succeeded finally in obtaining an engagement at the Metropolitan, around the corner, his first appearance being that of Walter in Raising the Wind. He returned to Maguire's where he was engaged for small parts. He rose to star in Davy Crockett, a romantic play of frontier life. Such was his success in this play that he traveled the country with it for years. It was revived in moving pictures with Dustin Farnum in the star role.

Lotta Crabtree was engaged by Maguire to play in his theatre at this time. At an earlier date Maguire had been shot at in the Square by Lotta's father because of a supposedly disparaging remark that Maguire had made concerning her abilities as an actress. Maguire never let personal antagonisms interfere with a chance to please the public.

"JACK PUDDING" COURTAINE

It was here, as early as 1857, that Maguire imported Harry Courtaine and his wife, Emma Grattan, from London. Courtaine had achieved fame as a light comedian, notably as Captain Maidenblush in The Little Treasure.* It was in this role that James Nesbitt, critic of The Bulletin, nearly broke

---

*The following paragraphs to page 24 are based on articles on Maguire by Pauline Jacobson, The Bulletin, Aug. 18-25, 1917.

Courtaine's heart by stating that he was a "jack pudding instead of a comedian." Such admiration had Maguire for Nesbitt's ability that whenever Nesbitt praised an actor, whatever Maguire's own judgement might be in the matter, he straightway called for the actor and raised his salary.

Courtaine was likewise notorious as a periodic drunkard, at which times, when he felt the spell upon him, he would lay aside his fine clothes and array himself in the habiliments of the tramp. Hardly had he been a month in town when he was seized with one of his periodic thirsts. Maguire cut it short by locking him in jail, but the company thinking him badly treated, bailed him out. Forthwith, upon his release, Courtaine proceeded on his spree. The next morning Maguire called his company together.

"Well, boys," he said: "you've seen fit to bail Courtaine out and to undo my work. You have done him a great injury. If you had known the character I received with him from London you might not have been so hasty. I cut him short, as I was advised to do it as the only means of keeping him at work. Your action has upset the whole business. Good morning." And Maguire turned on his heels in disgust.

COURTAINE'S FORTUNE

Courtaine remained in this city upwards of twenty years. His life here was passed by turns on the stage, in the gutter and the county jail, where he served his time out as trusty. He had a cell which he had pre-empted, and which was called by his name. He had an elegant figure, and his movements on the stage were grace itself. He was an accomplished linguist and musician. He sustained with credit, in his prime, the role of Figaro in The Barber of Seville and the Count in Il Trovatore, when those operas were given at Maguire's. Through drink he eventually landed in the dives and melodeons where he dragged his wife with him. Finally, she left him. His early life was a mystery. In view of his many accomplishments, credence was placed, above all other views, on the tale that he was the son of a dissolute Irish peer, the Marquis of Waterford. He died in rags on a street of the London slums.

OTHER NOTABLE IMPORTS

When the silver strike was made in Washoe, Maguire built a theatre in Virginia City which was opened by Julia Dean. This was another very successful theatrical venture.

In 1863 Maguire brought one of the most colorful figures in the theatre of that decade to San Francisco; this was Adah Isaacs Menken who achieved a tremendous success in Mazeppa both in San Francisco and Virginia City under his management.

It was Maguire who brought out Edwin Adams, Joe Jefferson; Charles Kean, the great English tragedian; Madame Celeste, the great French actress; and from Australia, the dashing Lady Don, who made her splendid success in Kenilworth. With her came Harry Edwards in his success as Mercutio in

Romeo and Juliet, and who became the founder and first president of the Bohemian Club.

Importing Edwin Adams was considered a great risk, but he proved to be the greatly beloved actor of his time. A tragedian famous in his day for his interpretations of Hamlet, Enoch Arden and of Robert Landry in The Dead Heart, he became a victim of consumption. At a benefit tendered him which netted $3000, the curtain disclosed him seated in a chair, for he was too ill to stand. He recovered a little in the milder climate of San Rafael where he lived some seven months. Soon after on his return East, he died.

It was Maguire who brought out Edwin Forrest, with John McCullough, as his leading man. Maguire expressed his desire to retain McCullough for his stock company.

"You can't pay me what I can get in New York," replied McCullough, not without a shade of contempt. "Who said anything about pay?" retorted Maguire. "How much do you want to stay?" "$150 a week," answered McCullough, which in those days, was a fancy salary for stock. "All right," said Maguire.

McCullough remained as leading man. Later as manager of the California Theatre, he took the majority of Maguire's company with him. Frank Mayo, Charles Thorne, Billy Barry, Lewis Aldrich and Sophie Edwin, however, remained loyal to Maguire to the end.

It was Maguire, who at great risk, brought out

Matilda Heron in <u>Camille</u>, a play considered at that time quite daring, for Matilda Heron, followed the French school of realistic interpretation. Maguire lost money on the venture as he did also on <u>The Black Crook</u>, a play likewise revived in the early days of the movies. The pulpits denounced <u>The Black Crook</u>, even more than <u>Camille</u> and Jack Lewin, a pioneer scene-shifter, has recorded that for the amazons in the grand march they had to gather in the women of the underworld, for to appear in tights was ribald, to be perpetrated only by women in the lowest burlesques. The bills announced Sallie Hinckley for the star part, and "an actual outlay of $12,000" for the "original grand, romantic, magical and spectacular" drama by C. M. Barras, entitled <u>The Black Crook</u>.

But Tom Maguire was never happy in any venture unless it had some element of risk. A born gambler, however big his loss, he was always ready to take another big chance. It was this that made him first in most things theatrical-- the first to bring out the great Booths, the first to bring out a Japanese troupe of acrobats, the first to import opera companies.

HIS LOVE FOR GRAND OPERA

There were two titanic conflicts in the sixties: The Civil War -- and Maguire's battles with his opera companies. His efforts to produce the most grandiose form of music brought about many stormy sessions both inside and outside his opera house, and eventually caused him great losses.

The new trend in San Francisco came around 1863 and seemed to strike Maguire with special force. He conceived a passion for opera -- its spectacular qualities must have attracted him -- and grew determined to put it across. Maguire, in the words of Johnny Ryan who was call boy at Maguire's and later on, clerk in the supervisors' office at the city hall, "was of the stuff of which trusts are made." He usually had two theatres going on at one time in the city; his opera house and the Metropolitan.

Later he replaced the Metropolitan with his Academy of Music which he built himself and designed principally as a temple of grand opera. At one time Maguire had a theatre in every big city in the state.

In 1855, upon the failure of Jerry Bryant and Orrin Dorman in the bank panic of that year, Maguire took over their San Francisco Hall of Minstrelsy, his first act being to build up the company by getting Billy Birch and the pick of Christy's men from the East. In time this company became famed as the greatest minstrel company in the country, taking even New York by storm in 1864.

In 1865 he changed the name of San Francisco Hall to Maguire's Opera House and enlarged it by two stories. In order to keep his minstrels going at the same time, he added his two stories by building around the original structure. He fitted up the interior in such a manner that it was said to be the handsomest outside New York.

MAGUIRE'S OP'RY HOUSE

"Maguire's," according to Johnny Ryan, "looked exactly like the Columbia Theatre, only not all that g-r-and gilt. There was fine cushions, but not all that velvet like in the Columbia, but fine cushioned chairs. It was lighted with chandeliers, but no electric lights. Everything was lighted by gas in them days. But no one didn't have any more elegant curtain. It was like a ballet dance. Oh, they ain't got no curtain in town like it.

"Maguire's one besetting sin was the love of grand opera. In those days the taste of the people did not run to the high class of entertainment, but he could not see it and insisted on getting the very best. If there was one constellation of stars that could shrink a bankroll, I believe an opera company took first rank. Events proved that Maguire could make more money out of a season with Alice Kingsbury in Fanchon, or Billy Birch's Minstrels, than he could with a dozen Brambillas, Mancusis and Parepa-Rosas put together; but he would have them and many a season left him broke, but not discouraged. He was not built that way."

At great cost, Maguire brought opera companies from the East by way of the Isthmus. He was very lavish. He plunged with salaries of $100 a night for a star and paid him $250 a week to wear his own costumes, Maguire not wishing to go to the trouble of furnishing costumes as the contract stipulated.

HIS FIRST IMPORTED OUTFIT

He imported the first complete Italian opera company, the Bianchi Opera Company with the first grand orchestra. Later he augmented the company with Gregg, baritone; Miller, basso; Brambilla, soprano; and Mancusi. They sang all of the old-timers -- beginning with La Sonnambula in a subscription season of eighteen performances. Signor Bianchi was found to be much the same as two years before, a sturdy and "rather fussy" figure, while Signora Bianchi was "as stout as ever -- perhaps a little stouter," with the same gushing style. Neither of the Bianchis was a particularly moving performer, but they were always "acceptable." The newspapers remarked that their supporting company had its faults, selecting in particular a Mr. Gregg, who admittedly boasted a fine voice but had peculiar mannerisms and an annoying habit of singing unintelligibly in English when he did not know the Italian words of his music.

According to some critics, Eugene Bianchi was a tenor almost without a peer at this time. He introduced the Paris Conservatory of Music pitch in this city.

> "At operas, between the acts," related August Wetterman who was conductor in this city since 1852, "Bianchi would come down to the music room with his tuning fork, the Paris Conservatory of Music pitch which had been founded upon the human voice. He hit the fork on his knee, then holding it to our ears, saying 'this is the right pitch. Gentlemen, you are all wrong. When I want to sing B flat you force me to sing B natural. This is outrageous. You must change your pitch or you will kill me.' "And we stood the abuse, narrated Wetterman, "knowing he was right."

GETTING HIS FILL

Maguire was getting his fill of grand opera. After conclusion of a season, opened on July 16, he announced another season beginning late in August. In the augmented company were included: the Bianchis, Mme. Biscaccianti, Messrs. Leach, Grossi, Roncovieri, Charles and Mme. Klebs. Light is thrown on the character of Maguire's audiences by the following comment in the Bulletin of August 26:

> "It may be interesting to those who do not attend 'the opera' to know that 'apples and peaches' are now regularly cried for sale among the fine ladies of the dress circle. Oranges and peanuts are as yet confined to the reserved seats in the parquette."

The Bianchis apparently did not get along with Maguire for their schedule was cancelled and on June 27 the Italian Opera Company commenced its own season at the American with Lucrezia Borgia (they played at intervals until August); but Maguire on the same day entered a legal complaint against Signor Bianchi, charging that Bianchi was using Maguire's musical scores, valued at $400, without permission.

Meanwhile, at the end of May, Maguire introduced an imported English opera troupe from New Orleans. He offered such locally popular operas as La Sonnambula, The Barber of Seville, The Bohemian Girl. After a successful month they gave place to Mr. Collins and Miss Fanny Morant (June 27), and Miss Avonia Jones (July 11-19). During the fall Maguire offered a succession of lesser importations including: Carrie, Sara and Alfred Nelson; Mr. and Mrs. George Sims, Mr. H. D. Thompson, Mr. Grosvenor, Carrie Howard, and, on December 26, the great Wizard of the North, Professor Anderson. Later on came trapeze artists and then a Professor G. A. Belew who tamed wild horses under the title of "The Great American Hippozanezapprivoiser."

MORE GRIEF WITH THE BIANCHIS

In May the Bianchis were appearing at the Metropolitan. Maguire, on May 2, announced a new imported operatic troupe which included Signorina Olivia Sconcia and Signors Orlandino and Sbriglia. Bianchi accepted the challenge of the new rivals, and for a time competition was keen. On May 3 the Bianchis gave La Traviata; the next night the new troupe followed suit. Completing their first subscription season of twelve operas on May 11, the Bianchis announced a new season and furiously rehearsed a new opera, Faust, which they presented rather hurriedly on May 17, with the San Francisco Mannerchor assisting. On May 25 the Academy of Music company offered, for the first time in California, Un Ballo en Maschera. On the following night the Bianchis gave the same work.

It was early in June when the Bianchis finally came to grief and the operatic season to a "premature close." The explanation was found in a "card" published in the newspapers, which read as follows:

> "Having not received the salary due to me for eight days past, from the Impresario of the Metropolitan Theatre, I have declined to sing TO-NIGHT, FRIDAY
> ELVIRA BRAMBILLA"

A week later Warwick, now stage manager at the

Academy of Music, announced that Maguire had engaged the principal stars of the Bianchi troupe and that the augmented company would continue to offer Italian opera to a not overly clamorous public. The Bulletin expressed doubts as to the financial stability of the venture. Although Maguire announced an advance in prices (now 50¢ to $2), the critic referred to the balance sheets for the week ending June 6, which showed a loss of $1,634 for the week. This pessimistic view seems to have been justified, for at the end of August, when Maguire finally closed the season, his losses were estimated at $20,000.

Bianchi and his wife remained here as singing teachers, and sometimes got up operatic performances. She was called "the mother of music" of this city. An only son survives, his home here, his wife a well-known singer.

DISASTROUS LOSSES

Maguire imported William Lyster of the English Opera Troupe, who gave all operas in English, with Rosalie Durand as prima donna; Hawison Opera Company; the Caroline Richings Opera Company and Mme. Euphrosyne Parepa-Rosa.

Parepa-Rosa was hailed with enthusiasm, but the receipts of the season were not sufficient to balance the enormous expenditures. Indeed, it was later stated that, while the prima donna left California several months later with a clear profit of $20,000, Maguire suffered heavily by his venture. Parepa-Rosa, it is said, was so fat that she looked like a bag tied in the middle and, because of the fat, you could not see where it was tied. But when she opened her mouth it was as if the gates of heaven were ajar. You forgot all about her fat, only noting the sweetness, power and wonder of her tone, which came like a musical brook, swelling on and on until it was like some mighty river. It is recorded that when she contracted measles it was necessary to close the theatre for a week.

Most disastrous to Maguire was the Adele Phillips opera season. A statement published in the <u>Alta</u> gives the loss of three opera nights as $1634, a weekly average expense of $4000 and the loss on the season as $30,000. The <u>Figaro</u> and <u>Dramatic Review</u> quoted in October 1868 an estimate that Maguire had lost in all $120,000 by his various operatic speculations.

INTERLUDE IN PARIS

His interest in opera remained in spite of reverses, and many years later we find Maguire visiting in Europe and becoming enthusiastic about French and Italian opera. We read in the <u>Morning Call</u>, dated August 18, 1878:

> "Mr. Thomas Maguire writes us from the Hotel des Etrangers, Rue de Trouchet, Paris, some of his impressions of the gay metropolis of the world, and also of the work he is doing in the way of procuring talent for Baldwin's. The letter is dated July 15th. He left New York on the same steamer with Kellogg and her mother, Strakosch, Gran, and Deutsch, and he speaks of Paris as if (seasoned veteran though he be) its sights and sounds bewildered him. He was

about to visit Milan and Rome, in company with Signor Verdi, to see some professionals personally with whom he had been negotiating by letter, and expected to return to New York by the steamer of the 8th of August. He had been at the Royal Italian Opera House every night in London, and heard the greatest prima donnas, tenors, bassos and baritones of which the world can boast! He discounts Patti somewhat in a vocal sense; has heard several with just as good voice, but none so pleasing as actresses. Mr. Maguire also witnessed the performance of <u>Carmen</u> -- the new opera which has a spice of naughtiness in it -- with Minnie Hauch in the title role, assisted by two other prime donne, three tenors, three baritones and three bassos, and to use his own language, he thinks the opera 'just the hit of the century.' But the surprise and admiration of the San Francisco manager were complete when he saw <u>Faust</u> performed at the Grand Opera House, Paris. He was open-mouthed with astonishment, and dumb from sheer delight. He has paid a good deal of money to Strakosch and other people to do this opera for the San Francisco public; but he is free to confess that he had never seen it until the occasion of which he writes, and then he irks that he cannot gratify his ambition to show his stay-at-home fellow-citizens what Gounod's work is really like. The desire was swelling within him, when, with his hat off, he stood on top of the Arc de Triomphe, one night, and saw Paris spread out before him, a star-lighted panorama of beauty. The manager has had his hat off a good many times since he has been in Paris. But he does not think the artists in Paris compare to those in London. The Parisians are fonder of spectacle and show than the Londoners. Mr. Maguire is in New York at present, and will probably reach here in the middle of September."

MORE OPERA

But Maguire, nothing daunted, continued to put on an opera till he lost his Academy of Music, and Baldwin, as has been said, had to stake him to his new theatre when his opera house was closed, on the widening of Kearny Street.

He sent his opera companies as far as Virginia City. It was the Caroline Richings Company that broke even only through the kindly intervention of the wind. A storm came up, which blew down the circus tent and sent all the people to shelter and the single other amusement in town -- the opera. From Pauline Jacobson, The Bulletin, Aug. 18, 1917:

> "Opera, opera, opera, people yell all the time for opera," complained a pioneer scene-shifter, "but the only one who comes is the four hundred and the Eye-talian fishermen. Most people haven't the price for even $2 in the gallery, while the four hundred come only for a few nights till their curiosity is satisfied, and the Eye-talian fishermen can't pay at all. The four hundred just go to rubber and talk, to see and be seen. The stage manager ordered all the lights out one night in the house just to keep 'em from rubberin' and talkin'. After a night or two they don't come no more.
>
> "The greatest butters-in on grand opera are the Eye-talian fishermen. They know their music, but they haven't the price. Whenever we wanted singers for the chorus and hadn't time to train them, we used to go down to the wharf and get the Eye-talian fishermen. You'd find every one of 'em knowing their score and singing Ernani and Traviata. You could only use a limited number, but every evening they'd crowd in at the stage door. 'I'm in the chorus! I'm in the chorus! they'd say. We'd know they wasn't but we'd let them in when nobody was looking.
>
> "You would think Tom Maguire would get discouraged," went on the scene-shifter. "What does he do but come in one day and, with the company starving to death in this city, ordered us to pack the scenery for Sacramento. 'They want opera in Sacramento,'he says excitedly. 'They've been yelling their heads off for weeks for opera.'
>
> "So, at great expense," wound up the scene-shifter, "we ships scenery and the Brambilla Company to Sacramento. The first night we took

in exactly $38. The next, not that. We ran two nights and closed up. All want opera but no one won't pay for it. All people will pay for is drama and vaudeville."

It is claimed that but for his love of grand opera, Maguire would have ended a rich man.

BATTLES WITH THE LAW

The old yields place to the new, and the later sixties brought important changes to San Francisco. The post-Civil War boom, the completion of the transcontinental railroad, and the general growth of the city brought a different atmosphere to it; its days of self-sufficiency and isolation from the East were ended. New influences were also affecting the whole dramatic scene. Tom Maguire was about to enter his period of decline.

SCANDAL SHEETS

Violent scandal sheets were popular at this time. One of their characteristics was to attack by innuendo, understatement, insinuation and open derogatory remark, the productions and producers of any theatre not advertising in them. Maguire became, for a time, the butt of constant ridicule, the Chronicle-Review being especially critical. When Maguire advertised in the Critic Figaro a little later, that paper immediately began to praise him in all his ventures.

An almost invariable corollary of theatrical pursuits -- from the days of the strolling mummers in pre-Shakespearean times, who were legally classified as vagabonds, to the bohemian thespians of today who often make the headlines -- is conflict with the law. Maguire had lots of court battles throughout his Napoleonic career. The newspapers of his time furnish us with interesting examples.

CRITICS SUED FOR SLANDER

There was the occasion when Maguire protested at court the libelous remarks of his critics. Following this, the Daily Dramatic Chronicle, published by M. H. and Charles de Young, informed their readers on August 2, 1866:

> "The proprietors of the Dramatic Chronicle have been arrested in a criminal proceeding for slander. The people of the State of California are nominally the aggrieved parties, as the offense is charged against their peace and dignity; but we understand the specific charge to be that we have wounded one Thomas Maguire in his good name, fame, and reputation; that we have injured him in the estimation of the community in which he has long resided; have tarnished that bright name he has heretofore borne among his neighbors and all good citizens, and other wrongs and injuries, the said Thomas Maguire then and there did, all of which is contrary to the statute in such case made and provided, and is against the peace and dignity of the community of California. Now, as to this last charge, it touches in a tender place. The Dramatic Chronicle is sensitive upon the points of dignity. We endeavor to preserve our dignity under all circumstances, and if we have done anything to lower our high standard, or let ourselves down in the estimation of the good people of this state, we ask their pardon. As to the allegation of breaking the peace of the state, we do sincerely hope that nothing serious will come of it; but if, like Austria, she, should be forced into an unwilling war, may victory perch upon her banners, and may the Rhine run within all her borders. As to that most estimable citizen and gentleman, Thomas Maguire, Esq., we hope we haven't hurt his feelings much, and we do not believe that we have

seriously offended the opinion which good citizens have heretofore entertained of him."

On Sept. 13, 1866, we learn the outcome of the case.

"The learned Judge Rix when he came to the conclusion that our libel case was altogether too deep a matter for him to say anything about, and accordingly sent it before the Grand Jury, fixed our bail at $2,500.00. The prosecuting attorney, thinking that the learned Judge may perhaps be slightly prejudiced, has reduced it from $2,500.00 to $5.00. Has, in fact, knocked off the odd thousands."

The feeling between the parties was still not altogether friendly. A hidden feud seems to have been carried on. The *Chronicle* of September 15, 1866, reports:

BENEFIT TO THOMAS MAGUIRE

"Lady Lou has offered to perform for the benefit of Thomas Maguire on one evening previous to the termination of her present engagement. Mr. Maguire has accepted her ladyship's favor in a polite note numbering twelve printed lines. The members of the Opera House Company also tendered their services free of charge on the occasion of this benefit. These forty ladies and gentlemen received a note numbering five printed lines. It was as follows:

> Opera House
> Sept. 10, 1866.
>
> Ladies and Gentlemen:
>
> Your favor is received. I accept your proffered services, and with much respect I remain
>
> Yours truly,
>
> Thomas Maguire.

"He might have said 'Thank you,' we think. Surely forty true-born American citizens, members of the dramatic profession, are equal to one member of the dramatic profession who married an English baronet who became an actor. We are afraid the manager of the opera house is becoming aristocratic in his notions and has an idea that those to whom he pays money for services rendered ought not to be treated with too much respect. However, Thomas Maguire is such an enterprising manager, and caters so well for the public amusement, that we hope he will have a capital benefit; the more money he makes, the more the public will be benefited."

And on Oct. 6, 1866, we read:

"A DISORDERLY HOUSE"

"On the reopening of Maguire's Academy of Music with a band of minstrels last Wednesday night a most disgraceful scene occurred. The management of Maguire's Academy of Music had engaged an Ethiopian performer named Billy Sheppard, who a few months ago killed a Mr. Ballou at Virginia City, and was acquitted of murder. On the appearance of Billy Sheppard on the stage, a tremendous uproar ensued; he was greeted with hooting and cries of murder, and on the stage, a large brick-bat was thrown at him. Policemen are always in attendance at Maguire's Academy of Music and after a time they succeeded in keeping the audience tolerably quiet."

"MAGUIRE'S JAPS"

Even the following year the Chronicle is critical of Maguire's ventures. It seems that Maguire brought several groups of Japanese acrobats to this country with great success. They all played in San Francisco and Maguire sent two of the companies on the road.

The following item appeared in the <u>Daily Dramatic Chronicle</u> for June 22, 1867:

"Accounts from New York say that the Japs still continue to draw big houses at the Academy of Music. So long as they do that Maguire will not take them to Paris or anywhere else. The left wing of the Japs is vibrating thru the principal towns under the management of Mr. Marshall. When the Japs are played out, we shall not be surprised to hear that Maguire has leased one of the Broadway theatres. Should he do so, Maguire will find out that managing a theatre in San Francisco and one in New York are entirely different affairs. There will be no opportunity for monopolizing all the theatres and all the talent in that vast section of the country, so he will have to content himself with managing one theatre at a time. We will no doubt be much surprised and gratified to find out how much easier it is to make money and keep it by running only one theatre at a time. The managerial policy of making money in one house and losing it in another is, in our opinion a very unwise and injudicious one, and is sure to prove serious in the end."

THE BLACK CROOK

An entertaining court battle took place between Maguire and Julien Martinetti, manager of the Metropolitan Theatre, in April 1867, in connection with the simultaneous production of two plays, one The Black Rook and the other The Black Crook.* The two plays were practically alike and it was apparent that one had been plagiarized from the other.

Martinetti claimed that his play The Black Rook was the original and that he had had it in rehearsal for some time before Maguire's production of The Black Crook. He said that he had given the script to an actor whose duty it was to make parts for the company and that the actor had sold a copy

---

*The following paragraphs, to page 43, are paraphrased from Annals of the San Francisco Stage (Federal Theatre, unpub. MSS.)

of the script to Maguire for $100.00. On this basis he sought an injunction against Maguire.

Maguire held that his play was the original and that he bought it directly from the playwright in New York. Retaliating, he asked for an injunction against Martinetti. While the court was trying to come to decision both bills played to crowded houses. Each was advertised "the one and only original."

BURLESQUE ON PLAGIARISTS

The Olympic Theatre took advantage of this controversy by presenting a burlesque called <u>The Black Hook with a Crook</u>. Their ad in the Daily Dramatic Chronicle read as follows:

> "Tonight for the first time in California will be presented the unstolen copy of "The Black Hook with a Crook." And the public may rest assured that there will be no injunction as this wonderful scenic spectacle has been arranged expressly for this theatre by Mercury, the God of Thieves."

MRS. GRUNDY IN COURT

Neither Maguire nor Martinetti succeeded in foiling each other thru the courts. Injunctions were denied to both. The Judge found Maguire's play to be the original but denied both pleas on the grounds that neither play was fit to be performed in public. His decision reads in part:

> "This court does not pretend to be the conservator of the public morals; that is a matter for the local legislature. But in giving construction to the constitution and the laws, when

> legitimately called upon to do so, it is the duty of all courts to uphold public virtue and discourage everything that tends to impair it. It cannot be denied that this spectacle of 'The Black Crook' merely panders to the pernicious curiosity of very questionable exhibitions of the female person. The lawfulness of such an exhibition depends upon the laws of the place where it is exhibited; but when the author or proprietor of the spectacle asks for the powers of this court to protect him in the exclusive right to make such an exhibition under the copyright laws of Congress, the matter assumes a very different aspect. I am strongly impressed with the conviction that an injunction should not be allowed in this case, on the grounds that the spectacle is not suited for public representation, neither in the meaning of that word as used in the Act of Congress, nor on the further ground that it is not within the scope of the power of Congress to encourage the production of such exhibitions, as neither promote the progress of science, or the useful arts."

This is a piece of dramatic criticism and recommends censorship, but hardly an answer to Maguire's request for an injunction. Of these three shows <u>The Black Rook</u> was the most successful, having had the longest run. Its success was largely due to the chorus of "80 beautiful girls."

VESTVALI THE MAGNIFICENT

The first hint of conflict between Maguire and his new lady star, the magnificent Vestvali, was reported in the <u>Bulletin</u> on Oct. 27, 1866. The article said in part:

> "MANAGERIAL TROUBLES -- Thomas Maguire was arrested yesterday upon the complaint of 'Vestvali, the Magnificent,' on the charge of making threats against her person, from which she alleges that she stands in fear of said Maguire...Her complaint alleges that he threatened that he would break every bone in deponent's body before deponent shall leave the

city, and in making said threat used the following language, to wit: 'You damned fiend under the mask of a woman, (repeated three times, with violence and gesticulations) take care; you have come to the right man. I'll prove that you have bones in your flesh, and before you leave the country I'll break every bone in your body'...The complaint is signed in a masculine style of handwriting, 'Felicite de Vestvali,' with a business-like quirl underneath..."

Vestvali's suit against Maguire was for $30,000. The lady claimed that according to her contract she was to receive half the receipts of the house above $250, one hundred nights' engagement plus twelve and a half clear benefits. According to the <u>Bulletin</u> of October 31, 1866:

"Vestvali says she has fulfilled her part of the contract in every particular. She alleges that Maguire and his stage manager, Graves, have put many obstacles in the way of her success. She also alleges that Maguire has acted contrary to all theatrical precedent in engaging Bandman, George C. Boniface and Miss Emily Thorne during the time of the plaintiff's engagement, all of which is against the wishes of plaintiff. She alleges that she recovered from her illness on the 1st of October, since which time she has been ready and willing to play, but was prevented by Maguire...She alleges that she might have remained in New York at $250 per night, in gold coin, but came here on the representation of Maguire's agent and wife, who assured her that Matilda Heron made $50,000.00 to $60,000 during her visit here, and that she should be supported by Charles Wheatleigh as a stock actor at $100 per week, and other alleged false representations."

It is difficult to determine the merits of this case which, it seems, was dismissed on Maguire's promise not to carry out his threat!

<u>PIRATE BROUGHT TO BAY</u>

Arrested for pirating plays, Maguire experienced a

slightly harsher contact with the law according to the <u>Daily Examiner</u> of Dec. 19, 1880:

> "The arrest of Thomas Maguire in New York for pirating plays, and otherwise gaining money by others' brains, is looked upon with interest by the dramatic, musical, and dramatic authors' fraternity. Bartley Campbell is determined to see that the law is enforced, and is willing to spend $10,000 for Maguire's conviction.
>
> "Authors both in London and America will contribute towards the fund for the prosecution. Maguire has for years defied the law that gives authors a share of the profit derived from their works. The latest plays from London have been performed here, and it is a well known fact that some one has stolen all these works for Maguire. Any attempt to enforce the law has hitherto been unavailing. There are now a number of unsatisfied judgments out against Maguire, who has carried on the business of play-pilfering for the past five years. Whenever he was sued he simply stated that his nephew Charles Goodwin, was the manager and he only the agent. If Goodwin was sued some one else was the manager, and so on ad lib. It is said that A. M. Palmer, James S. Mackaye and several other well-known managers will give most damaging evidence against him. 'French Flats' was obtained by Maguire from Palmer by false pretenses and the royalty never paid for. The agent of Palmer never had the MS. returned to him. At any rate, Maguire is under $7,000 bail, which may teach dishonestly inclined managers that there is a law in the land which can be invoked upon even a 'veteran' manager's head."

These examples of conflict with the law would seem to indicate that our back-stage Napoleon had ample opportunity during his checkered career to front and affront the courts of California. He seems to have done so with impunity.

THE DECLINE OF TOM MAGUIRE

Maguire on Hamlet

One of the more interesting anecdotes about Maguire tells of an interview which took place in the early seventies. It seems that a reporter from the <u>Alta California</u> called on our aging Napoleon at the Baldwin Theatre and announced that he would like to sell him a play.

"Well, my boy," said Maguire,"I'm bothered to pieces with new plays." "But let me tell you the plot," persisted the journalist. Maguire hated like the deuce to hear the infernal tiresome plot, but as the reporter had considerable influence with the press, determined to be civil to him, and told him to sail ahead. "Well, in the first act there is a man who goes crazy." "Ah," said Maguire, "a daftman is a dead weight to a play; the insanity should be wholly confined to the author. How did he get cranky?" "He thought someone had killed his father, and accused his uncle of it." "Oh, I see. Then the detective gets to work on the clue. Of course you have a detective?" "Oh, he does the detective business himself." "That's bad. How in blazes could a crazy man work up a clue? You must change that, and lug in a detective of the Hawkshaw pattern. What next?" "Well, his uncle marries his mother." "Now, here, Cap., we can't stand that business at Baldwin's. Every time we try an immoral snap, we catch it from all sides. You must cut out the part of the uncle. It's good, sensational, but won't do." Then the crazy man takes the family to a theatre, and gets the actors to ring in a scene that will remind the uncle of the murder." "All bosh, my boy. If a man should come to the theatre and ask such an absurd favor, he would be kicked out of the side door by the scene-shifter. There's nothing in it. Besides, how did he know his dad was salted if he didn't see it?" "Oh, I fix that, his father's ghost tells him." Here Maguire broke into a fit of laughter. "That's dead rot, these blasted ghosts are too old-fashioned for the stage. That won't work. Cut the ghost, my boy; cut the ghost." "Then he falls in love with a young girl who goes and drowns herself, being crazy, too." "Two cranky people in one piece won't work. You must shelve the girl." "Then they bury the girl, and at the funeral the crazy man has a row with the girl's brother and licks the officiating clergyman." "Hold on. Don't put such rot as this in. It will be hissed off the stage. A row at a funeral don't take anyhow." "Then the brother and the crazy fellow have a duel; he kills his man; the old lady takes poison, then he kills his uncle and...." "Say, young man, pause; I've heard quite enough. This is the most infernal and confounded rot I ever heard of. They wouldn't play it in a melodeon. What the devil do you call all this blasted trash?" "Hamlet," said the reporter, without a change of countenance and then he vanished through the door.

The language employed by Maguire to express his feelings is not recorded.

BENEFITS AND TESTIMONIALS.

While the precarious nature of theatrical enterprise may necessitate periodic appeals to public support on the part of veterans in the game who have fallen on evil days, it may also be possible that a profusion of benefits and testimonials given to an individual -- Tom Maguire in this case -- would indicate a gradual weakening of his legitimate drawing power, a loss of general interest, a hardening of the arteries, and an approach of inevitable decline. San Franciscans have always been generous to aging theatrical personages. The following excerpts from the journals of the day give one a vivid feeling of this. First we find in the files of Figaro of 1868:

"July 22. A GRAND BENEFIT FOR NAPOLEON. All must confess that California is peculiarly happy in the possession of such a theatrical manager as Thomas Maguire, who has so richly earned the title of 'The Napoleon of the Pacific Stage.' Spasmodic attempts are ever and again made to inaugurate theatrical enterprises in opposition to him, but they are rarely successful. The public have learned that their sole dependence on seeing the great stars of the present age must rest in him, and never once has their confidence in his tact and energy been betrayed. Mr. Maguire is about entering upon the greatest enterprise which he has yet undertaken -- the giving of a season of Italian Opera on a scale which has seldom, if ever, been attempted anywhere in the United States outside of New York City. Under these circumstances, it is eminently fitting that the public should strengthen his hands and provide him with the sinews of war. Therefore it is contemplated before the commencement of the Italian Opera Season to give Mr. Maguire such a complimentary benefit as was never before given to a theatrical manager. An entertainment will be given at Maguire's Opera House and at the Metropolitan Theatre on the same night. All the chief dramatic and musical talent of the State will, on that evening volunteer their services and the occasion will be worthy of one who has been so indefatigable in his efforts to build up the drama in California as has Manager Maguire."

LETTER OF APPRECIATION

San Francisco, July 22, 1868.

T. Maguire, Esq.,

Dear Sir:

We take pleasure in hearing that your friends propose giving you a complimentary Benefit, and beg you, as a slight token of our appreciation of your successful efforts for the past 19 years as a Theatrical Manager in California, to accept our gratuitous services on that occasion; and hope the compliment offered will be followed by such a substantial realization as your energy and enterprise in Theatrical Management richly deserve. We subscribe ourselves,

Yours truly,

(Signed)

John McCullough	Gus Bilfinger
Sophie Edwin	Henry Edwards
Mrs. Judah	Willie Edouin
John Wilson	Clelia Howson
Wm. A. Mestayer	Joseph L. Schmidt
John King	H. Schreiner
Chas. Thornton	K. Poppenberg
Henry Coad	E. Schlotte
Helen Tracy	Fr. Stoehr
Kate Lane Lynch	Fr. Boehme
Madge H. Lynch	A. Muller
Wm. Simms	C. Fischer
Frank C. Deaves	P. Kohler
Martin M. Joyce	A. Hellwig
A. Kidd	H. Macklin
G. W. Colby	H. Stackhouse
Geo. T. Evans	John Neal
Mrs. Hall	J. Henly, Jr.
Mrs. Adams	Thomas Gossman
Mrs. Yonker	J. Snyder
Mrs. Weston	Eva Tracy
Mrs. Julia Gould Hall	Eva West
Fred Franks	W. Burbery
M. L. Franks	Geo. Bell
Edward Thayer	James Clark
Emma Howson	Lucille Western
Emily Dashwood	Lizzie Dashwood
Annie Jackson	G. Mancusi
Brookhouse Bowler	G. Pizzioli
P. Ferranti	G. Sforzani
Luisa De Ponti	D. Devivo
G. Reina	W. Fuller
Raphael De Solla	M. White

Messrs:

Swift	Carmani	Bark
Nordblum	Schwabel	Newman
E. Bourquin	White	Krefchman
Brown	Stevens	Hennecart
Loomis	McCabe	Harry Jackson
W. Stevenson		Sheridan Corbyn

"July 24. THE MAGUIRE TESTIMONIAL. The programme of the entertainment to be given at Maguire's Opera House and the Metropolitan Theatre on Monday evening next, when Thomas Maguire will be the recipient of a testimonial tendered him by the dramatic and musical profession in California, has not yet been announced.

There is no doubt but that it will be an immense one, San Francisco was never more rich in dramatic and musical talent than at the present time and every one will be glad to join in a testimonial to one who has really built up the drama on this coast. By the bye, with so many musical artistes in the city, could not the public be treated to just one act of Italian opera as a foretaste of the pleasure in store for them during the coming season? We are sure that this would prove gratifying to the public, and the preparations for the Opera Season are already so far advanced that very little rehearsal would be required."

"July 25. OTHELLO ON BENEFIT PROGRAM. As the chief lights of the dramatic and musical professions have volunteered on the occasion of the complimentary testimonial to Thomas Maguire, who is emphatically the theatrical manager of the Pacific Coast, on Monday evening, so will all who are at all interested in the progress of music and the drama on this coast be anxious to take part in it. How excellent a programme has been prepared for this occasion may be known when we mention that at the Opera House Othello will be given, with Mr. John McCullough in the title role, and Mr. Barrett as 'Iago' after which the charming Dashwood Sisters will appear in The Love of a Prince; and that at the Metropolitan Miss Lucille Western will appear in The Loan of a Lover, after which an interlude will be given in which the best talent of the Pacific Coast will appear, and the performance will conclude with the last act of Luisa Miller by the artistes engaged for the coming Italian Opera Season."

ANOTHER PRELIMINARY ANNOUNCEMENT

"July 27, 1868. THE MAGUIRE TESTIMONIAL: The public of San Francisco is noted for the liberality with which it treats any star performer who has given it pleasure. Nay, even if his performances have not been very well liked, they will give him a testimonial if he has done the stage some service. Tonight the public have an opportunity of testifying their appreciation of the efforts of the manager who has at various times introduced nearly all the stars of the day to the San Francisco public. If the public failed to appreciate what he has done for their amusement during a period of nineteen years, it would indeed be ungrateful. There is no fear of this. Both Maguire's Opera House and the Metropolitan Theatre will be crowded to their utmost tonight, when Thomas Maguire, the theatrical manager of the Pacific Coast, receives a testimonial tendered to him by the musical and dramatic profession. The programme for the evening is an excellent one. At the Opera House Othello will be played, with Mr. John McCullough in the title role, and Mr. Barrett as 'Iago.' Those who have never seen John McCullough's 'Othello' have missed one of the very best impersonations of that character ever given on any stage. After the tragedy, the charming Sisters Dashwood will appear in The Love of a Prince. At the Metropolitan, the entertainment will commence with A Loan of a Lover, with Miss Lucille Western as 'Gertrude;' after which a grand musical olio will be given by some of the finest musical artistes in the city, and the whole will conclude with the last act of Verdi's grand opera of Luisa Miller. The prices have not been raised above the usual rates, and a ticket for the evening admits to both houses."

A REVIEW OF THE BENEFIT

"July 28, 1868. MAGUIRE'S OPERA HOUSE. This house was crowded last night, when Thomas Maguire, the Napoleon of managers, was the recipient of a testimonial tendered him by the musical and theatrical professions of the Pacific Coast. Othello was played, with Mr. John McCullough as the Moor. Mr. McCullough excels in the impersonation of this character. In the first act he does not polish up his elocution to such a dazzling brightness as to entirely hide the rough soldier, as many actors do, and in not doing so fails to make a popular point. In the impassioned scenes, Mr. McCullough is really great; he raves as 'Othello' should rave, and altogether, gives a thoroughly consistent representation of the brave soldier, but uncultured man, maddened by the acts of a polished gentleman. Mr. Barrett's 'Iago' was a correct but painfully studied piece of acting. It is not necessary that a continued by-play of lifting of the eyebrows, shrugging of the shoulders, and little spasmodic starts should be kept up, but Mr. Barrett as 'Iago' and Mr. Jackson as 'Roderigo,' in the scene in the Senate chamber, evidently thought that their dumb show would add much to the effect of 'Othello's' speech. Miss Helen Tracy acted the part of 'Desdemona' very well and Mrs. Sophie Edwin, of course, brought down the house as 'Emilia.' Misses Emily and Lizzie Dashwood gained great applause in the burlesque entitled A Love of a Prince, which was given as an afterpiece.

"Tonight the popular comedy of Rosedale will be played for positively the last time. John McCullough will take a benefit on Friday night."

"REAL GENUINE ORIGINAL PIONEER"

The San Francisco News Letter of July 9, 1870 commented as follows:

"The benefit to Manager Maguire was a veritable ovation to a gentleman who has in the past twenty years done his unmitigated best to amuse the public, not merely of San Francisco, but all of California and Nevada. Since '49 he has directly built eight theatres on this coast among them the Opera House, the now demolished Academy of Music of this city, the Forrest Theatre in Sacramento, and a theatre in Virginia City. The existing Maguirean temple, and that in Sacramento were built in '55, the former on the site occupied by the old San Francisco Hall. Maguire is the genuine original Pioneer Manager of the coast; his first theatrical venture of importance was the erection in 1850 of the Jenny Lind Theatre, which flourished for some time on the spot now occupied by the City Hall."

The Morning Call commented for several days, as follows:

"June 23, 1878. Mr. Maguire is in Europe in search of novelties, and we may expect to hear from him ere long."

"July 7, 1878. Manager Maguire is still loitering in the Louvre, or doing the Trocadero in Paris. We may expect some novelties from his English and French list. Henry Irving, perhaps, or Patti -- ah!"

Under an article entitled "Operatic Reminiscences" the dramatic critic of the <u>Call</u> writes on April 13, 1879:

"Since the period of the gold discovery, the American people have become accustomed or addicted to 'seeing Europe,' and they embrace the opportunity of witnessing the grandest operas and listening to the most famous singers. And the San Franciscans are equally cultured to the refinements of these most equisite accomplishments and entertainments."

"No manager understands this better than Mr. Thomas Maguire. Nearly all the operatic companies we have had on this coast from the time of Barili-Thorne until the present have been the result of his enterprise, and with the exception of the Lyster Opera Troupe (an English company that arrived her 1859-60,) the money he has lost on these ventures would put all our savings banks in sound condition today. As we think of the names of Hayes, Bishop, Brambilla, Ghioni, Sconcia, Fabbri, Stella Bonheur, Escott, Biscaccianti, Caroline Richings, the Bianchis. Milleri, Morelli, Gregg, Lamberti, Mancusi, Kellogg, Cary De Murska, Zelda Sequin, Squires, Carleton, Maas, Brignoli, and a score or more other famous artists, we can estimate the share San Francisco has had of lyric novelty, and how largely we are indebted to Maguire for procuring it."

TOM: A MAN OF EXPERIENCE

"October 26, 1879. The Anniversary Benefit of Manager Thomas Maguire is fixed for Sunday next, Nov. 2nd. It is as usual, tendered him by the entire dramatic profession of San Francisco, and the bill provided for the occasion will embrace every grade of entertainment. We suppose it will be useless for us to descant on the claim Mr. Maguire has to public recognition, as the oldest, most fortunate, and at times, unfortunate, manager of the Pacific Coast. Maguire has passed through experiences that would make a volume more salable than Mark Twain's 'Innocents Abroad'; he has endured ordeals that would send weaker natures to the drugstore or to Meiggs' Wharf. We don't know but that he is at odds with Fortune now; but this does not dishearten him, nor prevent his stretching out after fresh enterprises in the future and giving the San Francisco public a further taste of that quality which for thirty years has furnished nearly all the stars, lyric and dramatic, to the delight of the public, and in nine cases out of ten, to the impoverishment of the impresario. If there be a dearth of exceptional talent now, it is the fault of professional training, and not of managerial enterprise. Maguire will tell you, pulling his mustache, 'Show me the actor who's got the talent, and I'll have him in San Francisco if money'll do it.' We hope this manager of thirty years standing will have a good benefit. If there be any deserving in long service, he is a prominent claimant."

DEPARTURE FOR THE EAST

"Oct. 31, 1880. Mr. Thomas Maguire left us on Friday morning for the East, to be 'in' at the 'Passion Play.' If prospects are bright for him it is possible he may remain in New York permanently, keeping up his connection with Baldwin's Theatre. In the meantime Mr. C.H. Goodwin, young in years, but thoroughly up in the theatrical business, will manage the theatre here, and so Mr. Maguire may be able to manipulate attractions for his own profit and for the benefit of San Francisco."

"Nov. 7, 1880. As long as Maguire, the most enterprising and improvident manager in the State, spent his afternoons pulling his mustache and smoothing his hair back, on the steps of the Baldwin, it seemed impossible to help recalling some little incident of the old days. Fancy the petite figure of Alice Kingsbury, begging the Napoleon of the stage modestly for an engagement. 'What can you do?' looking down upon the little face with its bright, dancing eyes. "I can play 'Fanchon.'" Maguire had heard that 'Fanchon' was Maggie Mitchell's piece, and Maggie Mitchell was also a little woman. 'Well, you're just about the same size, ain't you? All right. You can have one night at it, and if it goes, we'll see; if it don't, well you'll make some money anyhow.' And the little Fanchon, playing to a cold audience through the earlier portion of the play, struck their hearts in the shadow dance, and made $18,000."

FOOTLIGHT FLASH

S. F. Chronicle, May 4, 1884. "There is nothing the average theatrical manager understands so little about as the quality of success in a stage performance."

"It is open to serious question if Tom Maguire, for instance, ever sat a piece clear through, or if he ever watched his most expensive star or stock company for more than ten minutes. For some months at one time a young man was engaged in the Baldwin in very small parts. Maguire did not, it was supposed, know he was in the place. After he had played nearly a season Maguire happened to look in when the young gentleman had a little speech to make. The manager walked out in front. 'Who in thunder is that fellow? He makes the smoke rise from my back.'

"When Bandmann was coming, some five years ago or so, Maguire recalled to all the critics the fact that he had made $15,000 ten years before that. 'He is, by ---, the boss -- the greatest of them all. Don't tell me. He is an actor to the Queen's taste.'

"Bandmann made a bad failure; played to empty houses, came out and stormed the box office, and Maguire, tearing his mustache to pieces almost in his rage, blurted out: 'He's the - - - actor I ever saw. Who in blazes ever said he could act?'

"But Maguire is not the only manager who never saw a play, nor is he the worst of them."

DRUMMING UP ANOTHER BENEFIT

San Francisco Chronicle, May 18, 1884. "Thomas

Maguire has been out of theatrical management for some time. He has not been very successful and his friends have tendered their assistance to arrange a benefit for him. Few men have so many old friends as Maguire. With all his erratic management, he did a great deal to educate San Francisco to that point at which it now stands and which has won for it a great critical reputation in the Eastern States. His pluck commanded admiration when his misfortunes drove him down. He has spent fortunes in running theatres and fought his way through all sorts of difficulties and all his life he has retained the friendship of those who knew him well. In seeking relief from pressing pecuniary difficulties, he can with more justice than most beneficiaries claim the assistance of his theatrical friends, and he will consequently be able to present a bill on next Saturday and Sunday nights at the Baldwin Theatre which will draw the whole town. We have never had any more enterprising manager, and when he gave up, the stock company went with him. Tom Maguire has been losing very greatly lately and he has abstained from dabbling in his favorite hobby with a constancy that denotes sufficient reformation to justify a bumper benefit. The Saturday night bill will be Rhea and the company in their strongest play. On Sunday the Galley Slave and an olio with everybody in it."

HIS WATERLOO: THE PASSION PLAY

Perhaps the most famous dramatic controversy in the history of the American theatre took place in the spring of 1879. Lawsuits, as we have seen, furnished almost a steady diet for Tom Maguire during most of his career. Often ridiculous, on this occasion the affair ascended to the sublime.

For several months, Salmi Morse, a playwright, had been trying to obtain a production of his biblical drama, The Passion, a representation of the martyrdom of Christ. It was a spectacle of the Oberammergau type, done in a devout spirit.

At length, the wealthy owner of the Baldwin Hotel and Theatre, "Lucky" Baldwin, was induced to offer his financial backing and Maguire was persuaded to produce the piece. The cast, at the opening in the Grand Opera House on March 3, included members of the Baldwin Theatre Stock Company, 80 singers, and a full chorus. Jerome Hart recalls the cast as follows: Christus, James O'Neill; Pontius Pilate, Lewis Morrison; Simon, A. D. Bradley; Herod, S. W. Piercy; Judas Iscariot, King Hadley; Mother of Christ, Mary Wilkes; Herodias, Kate Denin; Salome, Olive West. William Seymour was the stage director, David Belasco the prompter.

REAPING A WHIRLWIND

It is strange to find that this production should have caused a great upheaval in local San Francisco circles and throughout the country, especially since, according to contemporary reports, the play was accepted in a reverent spirit by members of the cast as well as the audience. It is related that many spectators, overcome by the beauty and religious fervor of the performance, knelt and prayed throughout whole scenes; and that members of the cast were uplifted to the point of foreswearing worldly habits and thinking in terms of the life hereafter.

But the City Fathers and the more conservative citizens felt that The Passion was a subtle approach to blasphemy. Said the Call of March 16:

> "The Passion Play slowly won its way to popularity against much opposition, until the Supervisorial ordinance finally squelched Morse and his daring innovation on stage literature."

Indeed, the play was offered only for a week before it was reluctantly withdrawn in the face of advancing favor.

It is also reported that the play caused a great furor among the Jews and Irish Catholics of the city. According to David Belasco's account, a committee of citizens called on Maguire and "worked upon his credulous nature" until he believed that he was marked by the devil for sacrifice and would meet with instant death if he did not withdraw his play. So in a fever of fear he closed the theatre.

TEMPTATION AND PENALTY

His ever-keen business sense, however, got the better of him, and on April 15, Maguire and Morse boldly revived the Passion Play for Easter Week, evidently determined to put a newly made ordinance to test. Says the Call of April 16:

> "At the close of the performance of the Passion Play at the Grand Opera House last night, Officer Bradford arrested James O'Neill, the actor, upon a charge of misdemeanor committed in violating the ordinance which prohibits the personation of any scriptural character upon the stage of any theatre. This is understood to be a test case...The accused gave bail in the sum of $100."

A few days later James O'Neill, father of Eugene O'Neill, the Nobel prize-winning dramatist, and other actors in the cast, were brought into court and fined. The Passion Play was withdrawn on April 22 in deference to public opinion.

Mr. Morse was to take his now famous drama to New York, but his struggle there was equally difficult and he finally committed suicide before the play was given another production.

On May 5, Maguire moved his opera company to the Grand Opera House. Here on May 14, was presented, for the first time in the city, the now classic opera Carmen. The season closed on May 23. Neither poetry nor advertising had availed; the series of thirty-four performances had netted a loss of $20,000.

The failure with the Passion Play seems to mark a turning point in Tom's career. It changed his gambler's luck and affected public sentiment toward him. It was the beginning of the end.

PARTNERS AND PRETENDERS

Tom's luck had changed. He was losing his grip -- and the whole town felt sorry for him, for Maguire was a gallant loser. Financial calamities were upsetting the whole country. The year 1873 had seen a National depression; 1875 a local panic; and 1877, a final catastrophe. With the third tidal wave of disaster, bad times set in permanently, it seemed, and the good old days of theatre profits became a theme of fond recollection.

Before his hefty British Blondes departed, Maguire was offered a benefit, after which the Alta California sentimentally remarks:

"The great crowd in attendance last night testified to the sympathy felt by the public for Manager Maguire who has held on so bravely to his business when times were hard and it seemed as if daylight would never come again."

Maguire's ventures into legitimate drama at this time were less successful than those of his rivals, McCullough and Emerson. Critics and audiences were unresponsive.

DESPERATE STUNTS

To curry favor with the evil times, managers desperately tried all kinds of "novelty" stunts for attracting the public. Large illustrated display advertisements in newspapers were introduced -- some three or four columns wide and full length; finally, full-page displays and ballyhoo to match. Competition was fierce, but audiences, the object of the competition, proved hard to move. There were too many too obvious attempts to extract hard earned dollars, and Californians who had been quite impressed by the elusive quality of their silver, were most unwilling to part with it.

A DEAL WITH LUCKY BALDWIN

Fortunately, Maguire, in the midst of calamities, succeeded in interesting "Lucky" Baldwin, the famous San Francisco millionaire, in entering upon a theatrical enterprise. Together, they built the Baldwin Hotel and the Academy of Music in 1876. Baldwin and Maguire were never very friendly -- lions are solitary creatures -- and it was young David Belasco who became Tom's secretary and acted as go-between in their business dealings.

Winter, in his Life of Belasco, remarks with amusement the partnership in the enterprise of Baldwin, an ex-hostler, and Maguire, former cab-driver. He states that they were not on the best of terms and that Belasco served as intermediary in the negotiations, which were complicated by the fact that Maguire owned the land selected as a site and was listed on the bills as "proprietor" of the new house.

We quote from the Annals of the San Francisco Stage (MSS. unpub.) compiled by the Federal Theatre Project, 1937:

> "Baldwin's Academy of Music was a part of a huge architectural unit which eventually housed the ornate Baldwin Hotel as well as the theatre. This house was located on Market Street near Powell, then at some distance from any other theatre, and was to influence the southwesterly trend in the entertainment district.
>
> "The Baldwin building was six stories high and was surmounted by a large domed tower and a number of smaller ones from which flags fluttered on state occasions. The theatre was a marvel of elegant filigree and red plush, boasting elaborate and expensive fresco painting, a drop curtain of satin -- which was said to have cost $6,000 --, velvet draperies, and gilt scroll-work. Crystal chandeliers were said to have cost $1,600 apiece.
>
> "At the opening of this theatre on March 6, Thomas Maguire, still proprietor of the smaller Opera House and of the New Theatre, was installed as manager. The first attraction was Barry Sullivan in Richard III. James A. Herne was stage manager, Belasco his assistant and prompter, and in the cast are listed: James F. Cathcart, Miss A. A. Adams, Lewis F. James, and Mr. D. 'Belasco' who played Ratcliff. Sullivan's success astonished many. The Chronicle announced that his Richard 'is beyond a doubt the best that has been seen upon the California stage.'

THE HANDWRITING ON THE WALL

But the trend was still downward and Tom Maguire could decipher the handwriting on the wall in 1877. After spasmodic offerings at his three theatres during the first months of the year, he announced retrenchments. On April 1st he reported that his Opera House had been leased to **Billy Emerson** on a two-year lease, and was to be known as Emerson's Opera House. Here Emerson opened on April 23, offering his minstrels. On April 1st it was announced that the Alhambra was also to be re-titled. The Bush Street Theatre opened on April 7 under the management of Titus and Locke. The first offering was burlesque by the Salisbury Troubadours.

THE SHUT-DOWN OF BALDWIN'S

Baldwin's Academy had closed ingloriously by April, and young Belasco, former right-hand man of Maguire, had in February been enlisted by a new variety house known as Egyptian Hall to write, direct, and act in specialty plays in conjunction with "illusions." Maguire was deserted by fortune and the public.

On and off, however, Maguire continued to produce plays at the Baldwin until 1882. During this period the relations between Maguire and Baldwin became more and more strained. Baldwin was forced to cover heavy losses at the theatre and Maguire was continually gambling in an effort to keep the enterprise going. Baldwin finally withdrew his support and Maguire's management was at an end. From that time until his death in 1896, his activities in the theatre world became increasingly negligible.

EXILE IN THE EAST

Perhaps in order to change his luck, Maguire moved East in the early eighties. Reports of his progress there seem conflicting. For a while it appeared that he was about to conquer a new world, and we half expected our aging Napoleon to enthrone himself securely in his latest kingdom, the Broadway of New York.

We read in the Morning Call of San Francisco on July 20, 1884:

> "Ex-Manager Maguire has been absent in New York more than a fortnight. Some say that he intends to surprise our public with an unexpected attraction; some, that he will devote himself to a new line of business in the East."

And, digressing a little, we hear about his nephew's marriage the same year -- The Morning Call of November 16, 1884, reports:

> "Mr. James Thomas Maguire was married in New York, Nov. 3rd, to Miss Fannie Muhlner. Both the happy parties hail from San Francisco. The gentleman is a nephew of the veteran manager, Thomas Maguire, and for many years was his ablest assistant in carrying on business. He is very well known in this city and is much respected for his honesty and integrity of character, coupled with fine business qualities. Later he was the chief adjutant of Messrs. Barton and Hill in the management of the California, and, recently, has filled responsible positions in the box-offices of the leading theatres of New York."

NEW EXPECTATIONS

Maguire, like an old prospector who always expects

to make a strike in the next hill, had great hopes of opening a new theatre in 1886. We read in the Morning Call on April 4, 1886:

> "The prospect of another new theatre looms up vaguely in the dim future. It is to be built by Mr. Thomas Maguire of San Francisco, who says that it is to be the prettiest theatre in the United States, not excepting the Baldwin Theatre or the Denver Opera House. It is to be located somewhere on the upper part of Broadway, and will run as a combination house. Mr. Thomas Maguire Jr., is to be its manager. The Maguire family have already built eleven theatres. They have left San Francisco and have come to New York to stay. Work is to be commenced on the new theatre next fall."

Concerning this, an anonymous correspondent wrote to the Call on May 16, 1886:

> "I was very much surprised to find so many professionals from 'Frisco. Yesterday, I met the veteran Tom Maguire, and found him notwithstanding his age and the varied experiences of the past, as lively as a cricket, and brimful of hope for the future. Maguire says he has a proposition under consideration which he thinks will reap him a good harvest next season. He wishes to be kindly considered by old California friends."

And putting up a front to match his illusory prospects, Tom Maguire, now in his seventies, changed his address and improved his attire. According to the Call of June 27, 1886:

> "Mr. Tom Maguire has just moved into a magnificently furnished house on Thirty-third Street, New York. The California ex-manager is said to be the best dressed man in that city."

ALMS FOR OBLIVION

But nothing much came of this. His theatre did not

materialize, and gradually in the course of his last decade, the old man sank into obscurity, and from obscurity by degrees into want.

We know little of his final period, though doubtless there were places and people in New York to whom Tom Maguire and his accounts of his golden days in El Dorado were familiar, if not a bit tiresome. He drifted about for several years, an impoverished and half-forgotten veteran of the theatre, and like so many others of the clan, died in destitution.

ON THE DEATH OF TOM MAGUIRE

The *Argonaut* announced his passing on Jan. 27, 1896 in the following terms:

> "The dispatches brought the sad news, a few days ago, that Tom Maguire had died in destitution in New York, cared for in his last days by the Actor's Fund. The present generation of play-goers in San Francisco do not remember him -- indeed, he left this city about seventeen years ago -- but he was long a mighty factor in theatrical affairs here.
>
> "He came to San Francisco from New York in 1849, and is reputed to have made a fortune of one million dollars in the theatrical business, though the last dollar of it was gone before he died. He built the Jenny Lind Theatre -- the middle of the three buildings on Kearny Street, between Washington and Merchant, which were subsequently sold by him to the municipality and became the old City Hall -- in 1852, and two years later he erected Maguire's Opera House, on Washington Street, in which many of the world's greatest actors and actresses appeared under his management.
>
> "Maguire's misfortunes began with the building

of the Academy of Music on Pine Street in 1862. He failed to make the enterprise pay and never again attained to much prosperity, though he leased the Eureka Theatre on Montgomery Street, between Pine and California, and, finally before his departure for the East in 1878, managed Baldwin's Academy of Music, now the Baldwin Theatre. In New York he could do little better than here, and his last years were passed in poverty."

A few days before this, on January 21, the Bulletin gave an account of his death. George E. Barnes summarizes his career in the article and relates a few unknown episodes of his life:

THE DEAD NAPOLEON: A FINAL ACCOUNTING

"Tom Maguire Dies in Want. A long fight against the inevitable ended. Riches that took unto themselves the wings of the morning.

"The news of the death of ex-manager Thomas Maguire was wired yesterday from New York, together with the melancholy fact that he was utterly destitute in the closing hours of his life. Thomas Maguire came to San Francisco in 1849 from New York. His early life and occupation there are involved in mystery but the latter was of the humblest kind -- that of driving hack. After trying his hand at all the chances that turned up after his arrival on the Pacific Coast, he eventually drifted into the theatrical business and became very rich, especially from the profits of the old Opera House, on Washington Street; but principally, when the minstrels were there, if the truth must be told, from the returns of the Diana gambling rooms attached to it. It is a well-known fact that his partner in this concern, yet living in this city, paid him over a million of dollars in less than a year as his share in the gains from the gambling tables of the Diana. Some who are in doubt as to Mr. Maguire's being worth $600,000 when he left Washington Street to build the Academy of Music, on the north side of Pine Street, below Montgomery, may easily see from this fact how such a financial condition was possible. The cost of the Academy was $40,000. Huling Majors was his architect, but he was much opposed to the project, as was Maguire's first wife.

"Said Majors to him one day: 'Maguire, have you thought closely on the step you are taking in building this theatre?' 'Why do you ask that question? Have you not all the men, money and material you need? What I require of you is good work and in as short a space of time as possible.' 'Ah, well; that's all right. I asked you the question because the time will come, in my opinion, and shortly, too, after you have finished the building when you will be sorry you laid one stone upon another.'

"Maguire must have felt in his secret soul that Majors' words were prophetic. There was a glare in those nondescript eyes of his -- no one could tell their color -- as he looked at the plain-spoken architect, and with an extra tug at his mustache he walked up the street. It was a pretty theatre, but as Majors predicted, it soon passed out of his hands, and was converted to business uses. It is now owned by Mrs. Theodore Payne. The Bergez restaurant now occupies a portion of it.

"Maguire monopolized all the theatres in the city at one time; but his hold was broken when Ralston and his coterie built the old California for Messrs. Barrett and McCullough. Then he ceased to be called the dramatic Napoleon of the Pacific Coast, and after various attempts to catch on again, finally left San Francisco for New York. This was about twelve or fourteen years ago. His life in New York, up to the time of his death, was one long and despairing fight against the inevitable, with the odds terribly against the poor fellow. A few incidents in the life of the departed manager may serve, better than any other means, to show the character of the deceased.

"He was by no means a literati. He did not read Shakespeare -- very few managers do. When Forrest was playing at the Washington Street Opera House, Maguire hailed a friend passing the theatre's portals one day: 'Say, coming to see the old man tonight?' 'I don't know. What's the play?'

'Corrylanus. It's first rate. One of his own.'
'Do you mean to say Forrest wrote it?' 'Of course he did. He can do anything that man kin.'

"But although Maguire was not blessed with much book-learning he had a natural faculty that stood him fairly in place of it. He was a good judge of individuals. He was a great observer, and he looked quite through the deeds of men; but sometimes, it must be confessed, he did not look far enough and was egregiously taken in. He admitted himself in this plight once. It was the time of the opening of New Montgomery Street through to Howard by the Harpending party. Maguire was a theatrical manager who always transacted affairs on the sidewalk. You might as well have tried to get him inside a church as to enter an office for business purposes in a regular way.

"In the early part of his managerial career, after he had got through with the 'Jenny Lind,' afterwards the old city hall, now razed to the ground, and up to the time of the death of Broderick in 1859, Maguire took an active part in politics. He was an earnest partisan of the 'Mudsill' Senator, as the Chivs used to call Broderick, and his partisanship took the form of financial aid occasionally. The Napoleon had plenty of ready cash in those days, and politicians, most of them were then, and are now, generally impecunious. Broderick resided with the Maguire family in their living apartments over the old opera house on Washington Street. The politics of the time were rough, and they suited the 'boys' of the period better than they did the Committee of 1856, who reformed them in a measure.

"Maguire was a generous man in his own way. There came to him one day, when he was airing his hair and pulling his moustache on the sidewalk, north side of Washington Street, a poorly but cleanly dressed woman, and asked him for the use of his theatre on Sunday night to deliver a lecture on Spiritualism. At that time theatrical performances on the first day of the week were contrary to law.

"How much will the rent be?" asked the applicant. Maguire looked her all over -- sized her up, as the saying is -- and asked by way of reply: 'Got any money?' 'No; but I expect to make the rent and a trifle over, if you will be kind enough to let me have the house.' 'Oh, you can have the house fast enough. The rent is $50.' The lecture was advertised and delivered, and next day the lecturer came around with the money. 'How much did you take in?' asked Maguire. 'Sixty dollars,'the woman replied tendering the rent. 'Is that all? Well, I don't need the rent just now. You take that $50, add some attraction to the lecture, music or something, and probably you may do better next Sunday.'

"The second lecture drew considerably over $100, and when it was tendered to Maguire, he said in brusque but kindly way, 'Now my good woman, I advise you to take that money and buy yourself some good clothes. You may be able to give me the rent by and by, but I do not need it at present.' More than once the subject of this kindly act has related it in print out of gratitude toward the man who befriended her when she was in want, and when he might have been under fire for some cause or other.

"Maguire was a very handsome man in his early California days, with a figure well developed and as straight as a pike-handle. He dreaded the idea of death; by a single remark on his appearance you could send him to tea and toast and bed. Those who knew this fact used it occasionally for a practical joke on him. He married twice -- first in New York, and the second time here. His first wife was his brains, and guided him in all the practical affairs of life; his second was a graceful brunette of most shapely figure and perfect shoulders. It was said of her that she was the only woman in San Francisco of her day who could wear a shawl properly.

"Mr. Maguire's age is given in the dispatches as about 70 -- he must have been nearer 80. It was a subject of which he was as tender as a woman, and never cared to have his age referred to...He had many faults, it is true, due mostly to the disadvantages under which he labored. Had Maguire been an educated man, he would have been a better one. He had some virtues. Let us weigh his virtues against his faults and judge him not too harshly."

PARTING WORDS: FINAL EVALUATION

There's little to add. We have reviewed our backstage Napoleon's career. We have learned of his early gambling saloon ventures, his difficulties with the Jenny Lind, his high-handed monopolizing of California's theatres, and of his passion for grand opera.

Passing the high climacteric of his Napoleonic decade, he becomes embroiled with law, we have found, and sues and is sued in turn by unsympathetic critics. He is given many testimonials and benefits and many times flirts with ruin. After a rather unsatisfactory partnership with Lucky Baldwin and the unfortunate incident of the <u>Passion Play</u>, he starts his downward path toward oblivion, being eclipsed by younger men, such as Belasco and Hammerstein. Going into a kind of exile in the East -- far from the scenes of his former triumph -- he begins in New York, we have seen, his final decade of decline.

A gambler-born and living by the gambler's code, Tom Maguire boldly pursued Dame Fortune all his life, whether she simpered at him or gave him the gate. In other circumstances, Tom might have become an East Side ward politician, a Chicago racketeer, a Florida land speculator, or a Hollywood movie-producer. As it happened, he found himself amidst the clamoring, pleasure-hungry population of a new El Dorado, and seizing his chances, he furnished it with spectacles, sensation plays, blood-and-thunder "mellerdrammers," minstrel shows, grand operas and ballets, making and losing several fortunes in doing so. Without a peer in the West, Tom Maguire earned his title: the Napoleon of Impresarios.

TOM MAGUIRE'S PROGRESS

1845	Hack Driver in New York
1846	Bar-tender in Park Theatre, N. Y.
1847	Saloon keeper at City Hall Place, N. Y.
1849	Comes to San Francisco during gold rush and opens gambling saloon, Parker House
1850	Builds on top of saloon his first theatre, the Jenny Lind -- soon destroyed by fire
1851	Second Jenny Lind razed by fire; he rebuilds it promptly
1852	Sells his third Jenny Lind for $200,000 to City Fathers for use as City Hall
1855	Assumes control of theatres in many small gold rush towns
1858	Becomes Napoleon of impresarios in California and theatrical monopolist
1860-70	Engages and imports such stars as John McCullough, Charles Thorne, Frank Mayo, the Booths, Mrs. Judah, Mrs. Saunders, Billy Barry, Harry Courtaine, Edwin Adams, Joe Jefferson, Charles Kean, Mme. Celeste, Harry Edwards, Edwin Forrest, Charles Wheatleigh, Januschek, Modjeska, etc.
1863	Conceives a passion for grand opera, builds Academy of Music as its temple, and imports opera companies, Bianchi, Harrison, Brambilla, Caroline Ritchings, and the English Opera Troupe, losing a fortune on these ventures
1866	Arrested for Breach of Contract and for making bodily threats against Mme. Vestvali the Magnificent.
1866	Sues his critics, the proprietors of the _Dramtic Chronicle_, for slander
1867	Charged with stealing and plagiarizing popular play _The Black Crook_
1868-70	Given a series of complimentary benefits and testimonials.

1873-75	National depression affects local theatre world; Maguire on the verge of ruin
1876	Enters in partnership with "Lucky" Baldwin, famous San Francisco millionaire and builds new theatre and Academy
1877	Baldwin's Academy which he manages, proves unprofitable
1878	Tours Europe in search of talent for Baldwin's
1879	Meets his Waterloo in <u>Passion Play</u> which arouses furious religious controversy and turns public sentiment against him
1880	Goes to New York planning to enter new line of business
1884	In great financial difficulties; San Francisco gives him benefit performance
1886	Negotiates to build new theatre in New York, unsuccessfully
1886-96	A decade of decline and gradual destitution in the East
1896	Dies in New York, cared for in his last days by the Actor's Fund

-----

TOM MAGUIRE

BIBLIOGRAPHY

Coad, Oral Sumner. *The Pageant of America.* (New Haven, Yale University Press. vol. 14, p. 181).

Foster, Lois M. *Annals of the San Francisco Stage.* (Mss. unpub. Federal Theatre, San Francisco 1937).

Hart, Jerome. *In Our Second Century.* (San Francisco, Pioneer Press, 1931).

Neville, Amelia. *The Fantastic City.* (Boston, Houghton Mifflin, 1932).

Rourke, Constance. *Troupers of the Gold Coast.* (New York, Harcourt, Brace & Company, 1928. pp. 31-33).

Winter, William. *Life of David Belasco.* (New York, Moffatt, Yard & Company, 1918).

Young, John Phillip. *San Francisco, A History* (San Francisco, S. J. Clark Publishing Company, 1912).

NEWSPAPERS AND PERIODICALS

Alta California	(San Francisco), August 24, 1864.
The Argonaut	(San Francisco), January 27, 1896.
Daily Dramatic Chronicle	(San Francisco), June 22, Aug. 2, Sept. 15, Oct. 6, 1866.
Figaro	(San Francisco), July 22, 24, 27, 28, 1868.
The News Letter	(San Francisco), July 9, 1870.
The Evening Bulletin	(San Francisco), June 2, 1863; Oct. 27, 1866; Jan. 21, 1896; Aug. 18, 25, 1917.
The San Francisco Chronicle	May 4, 18, 1884.
The San Francisco Herald	June 26, 1851.
The Morning Call	(San Francisco), June 23, 1878; Apr. 13, 1879; Oct. 31, 1880; Nov. 7, 13, 1881; April 4, May 16, 1886.

TABLE OF CONTENTS

DR. DAVID G. (YANKEE) ROBINSON

	PAGES
THE PIONEER OF DRAMA IN SAN FRANCISCO	72-108

Early Years	73
Advent into San Francisco	73
The Dramatic Museum	74
Premiere Performance	75
Favorite Songs	76
Repertoire and Cast	78
Benefit Performance	80
Siege of Cholera	81
Dramatic Museum's Busy Period	83
Novelty Presentations	84
Company Criticized	85
Robinson as Politician	86
A New Theatre	88
New Building Erected	89
Theatrical Competition	91
American Theatre Opens	91
Robinson-Stark Feud	93
Telegraph Hill Home	95
Robinson-Maguire Reconciliation	96
Coming of Lola Montez	98
Original Lola Burlesque	99
Manages Sue Robinson	101
Lotta-Sue Rivalry	102
New and Original Burlesque	103
Career Abruptly Ended	104
Leaves Vivid Memories	105
Representative Parts	107
Theatres Associated with Doctor Robinson	107
Bibliography of Dr. Robinson's Works	107
Bibliography	108

DAVID G. (YANKEE) ROBINSON
(1805? d. 1856)

BOOTH   ROBINSON

Dr. Robinson is shown here with Junius Brutus Booth, Jr.

PHOTO FROM THE SAN FRANCISCO CALL-BULLETIN.

DR. DAVID G. (YANKEE) ROBINSON
The Pioneer of Drama in San Francisco

The Gold Rush of 1849 brought to San Francisco a veritable horde of fortune-seekers, the majority of whom had ambitious dreams of acquiring wealth by the actual digging of the yellow nuggets from the earth. There were other fortune-seekers who had no thought of prospecting for gold in its natural state. They preferred (as a surer means of attaining wealth) to enter some sort of enterprise catering to those who did the actual mining. Prominent in this group of entrepreneurs were those who catered to the luxury and the leisure time desires of the new community; namely the entertainers.

But in spite of this influx of entertainers, and no doubt self-termed in the majority of cases, the stage in San Francisco was barren. The two theatres present in San Francisco at this time were mere tent structures with benches on the bare ground for spectators who had to be satisfied with acrobatics on spring boards or horseback.

Into San Francisco then, a town where the theatre had an audience but no drama, came an angular little figure titled "Dr." who had his own ideas of what the town desired in the way of drama. He was not the only figure in the entertainment world to bear this title, nor even the first, yet it was undoubtedly he who gave this title the aura and color it still retains as a nostalgic reminder of the days when the theatre was young.

EARLY YEARS

It is not strange that so little is known of Dr. Robinson prior to his advent into San Francisco on January 1, 1849. A New Englander, he was a road-show trouper, a playwright and manager and was reputed to have once, in his early days, worked with the great Barnum, the circus manager who had brought Jenny Lind to this country. Dr. Robinson was born in East Monmouth, Maine, between the years 1805 and 1809. His father, Jesse Robinson, had come to California about the year 1800 where he met and married a widow by the name of Clark. After their marriage they went back East to Monmouth where David was born. Dr. Robinson attended Yale University and was graduated as a physician between 1830 and 1835. There was no background of theatricals, stage or actors in the family which might have given the pioneer showman the initial incentive to enter the theatrical profession in San Francisco. He had come to San Francisco in 1847 as a doctor and established a drugstore in Portsmouth Plaza. It was while operating this drugstore in partnership with his brothers-in-law, Orrin and Evan Dorman, that a friend approached him on the subject of theatricals. A paternal ancestor, Dr. John Robinson, was credited with having sent the Mayflower to America. His grandfather Robinson had served in Braddock's ill-fated army and was also present at the Battle of Bunker Hill fighting on the American side.

ADVENT INTO SAN FRANCISCO

Quietly enough, Dr. Robinson entered San Francisco but immediately upon his arrival he made alterations in a small hall which he found in a little side street, putting up a low stage and contriving his own back drops and curtains. The ingenuity of an old trouper came to the fore when he found paints scarce in the pioneer town. His search for substitutes and pigment failing, he used mustard and curry instead of chrome yellow to color his back drop. Thereafter this single thick and sickly hue formed the background for all theatrical ventures on this stage. Here he gave Yankee impersonations in competition with Steve Massett until the great fire of May 1850 which all but razed the whole city of San Francisco. In partnership with the popular comedian, James Evrard, former manager of the English portions of the National Theatre Shows (and sometimes female impersonator) who later became a sergeant in the local police force, Dr. Robinson opened the Robinson and Evrard Dramatic Museum on California Street just below Kearny.

THE DRAMATIC MUSEUM

This playhouse was most attractive to the audience, and seating 280, it was filled nightly. A local newspaper boasted that people were turned away from the door an hour before the curtain was scheduled to rise. Whether as a deliberate bid for advertising or not, the Evening Picayune of August 7, 1850 carried a short story of the Dramatic Museum:

> "We visited, last evening, the Museum of Messrs. Robinson and Evrard, and take pleasure in expressing the satisfaction we derived. The performance was diversified, consisting of farces, songs, dances, etc., and were highly creditable and entertaining....The people of this city are not generally aware that such a place of amusement is in existence, or the house would be crowded at every performance. We commend it to the favorable consideration of all who desire to spend a pleasant evening."

Two days later, the Picayune carried the following ad:

A M U S E M E N T S

Robinson & Evrards
DRAMATIC MUSEUM, open every
evening, (Sundays excepted)

Pleasing Entertainments Nightly

Doors open at 7½, curtain rises at 8 o'clock.

Admission:
Private Boxes........$3
Upper seats..........$2
Lower seats..........$1

This was the first theatrical or amusement ad to appear in any San Francisco paper. A month later, an identical ad began appearing in the Daily Alta California.

The Museum's featured players were Mrs. Burrill, who subsequently acquired great local fame and popularity, and Mme. Duprez. While casting for his first production Robinson found actors scarce, but this proved no handicap to the resourceful trouper. He became the first dramatic coach in California, engaging a group of willing amateurs, training and coaching them, and making the most of their local connections in songs or parts. They proved to be an immediate and sensational success.

PREMIERE PERFORMANCE

His first play, "Seeing the Elephant"* was a loose

---

*In the popular phrase of that time, "to see the elephant" was to go to California expecting streets paved with gold and good luck as a matter of course and to be overwhelmingly disappointed and deceived by fortune. All the hard luck—rough travel, cold, hunger, bears and bandits, finding slim pickings—these were "seeing the elephant." The phrase was to be found everywhere—elephants appeared on letter paper, on miners' cabins, and illuminated that credo of morals known as "The Miner's Ten Commandments."

sketch, or rather a skeletal plot about which an enterprising manager could adapt a production almost limitless in its entertainment scope. This, Dr. Robinson did. The play had first been given in New York to ridicule the gold rush and had been given once before in San Francisco but without any attempt to adapt it to the California scene, which, after all, was the locale of the story. Dr. Robinson laid the plot in San Francisco, gave it many local implications, and with the added box-office appeal of a local cast, burlesqued nightly, to a full house, the role of the distraught and disappointed Yankee, Seth Slopes, who was the protagonist of the skit.

From the opening night on the Fourth of July, 1850 which climaxed a day of celebration including the annual erection of a new flag pole in Portsmouth Plaza, the Dramatic Museum was crowded. Miners of the region and local townspeople fairly fought their way to see themselves caricatured and to see and hear Dr. Robinson. He was not handsome, but his angular figure, hawk-like eyes and infectious smile lent themselves well to burlesquing well-known figures without malice but with rich humor. His knack for depicting character, a rich dialect, a well-nigh inexhaustible spirit, and an impression of acting for his own amusement made his impersonation of the shrewd Yankee as a farmer or miner outstanding.

FAVORITE SONGS

His song and pantomime act, "The Old Umbrella," was so popular and well-known that if he dared appear on the stage to sing it without the actual old ragged umbrella, the audience clamored till Dr. Robinson returned with it and an apologetic smile, another sign of his expert showmanship. His "Used-up Miner," sung in a wailing drawl, so captured the public's fancy that it became a favorite throughout the mining districts. Miners and adventurers of all shades of success and degrees of fortune throughout the land sang after him:

>Oh, I ha'n't got no home, nor nothing else, I s'pose,
>Misfortune seems to follow me wherever I goes,
>I come to California with a heart both stout and bold
>And I've been up to the diggin's there to get some lumps of gold.
>
>Oh, I'm a used-up man, a perfect used-up man,
>And if ever I get home again,
>I'll stay there if I can.
>
>I lives down in Maine, where I heard about the diggin's,
>So I slipped aboard a darned old barque commanded by Joe Higgins.
>I sold my little farm, and from wife and children parted,
>And off to California sailed and left'em broken-hearted.
>
>And here's a used-up man, a perfect used-up man,
>And if ever I get home again,
>I'll stay there if I can.

As performances progressed nightly, Robinson relied more and more on the local scene and began introducing well known California figures in rhyme. He now told his Yankee stories under the name of Hezekiah Pickerall. While he was undoubtedly the first dramatic coach in California, he was also possibly the first satirist in San Francisco, portraying every political figure. His "Random Rhymes" satirizing the municipal officers gained him such great popularity that he was made alderman in 1850 and was later named as the most popular candidate for mayor.

REPERTOIRE AND CAST

The Dramatic Museum's repertoire consisted largely of plays which were written by the doctor himself. The August 13th *Picayune* makes a very favorable mention of one of his plays:

> "Robinson and Evrard had a crowded house last night, which was well merited on their part. Their entertainment was highly interesting. Tonight a new piece will be performed for the first time, written by Dr. Robinson, entitled 'The Victim.' Something good may be expected."

Three days later, a critical review of this piece appeared in the same journal along with a bid for respectable patronage:

> "'The Victim' will be repeated this evening at Robinson and Evrard's. It is a highly creditable production of Dr. Robinson, and is well performed at the Dramatic Museum. The moral of the piece is not the least of its many merits..
> ...This place of amusement is well worthy of patronage of the respectable portion of our city. Everything connected with it is conducted with the most perfect propriety, and neat private boxes have recently been fitted up and tastefully furnished for the accommodation of lady visitors, a number of whom grace them with their presence."

The dynamic doctor was losing no time in producing on the stage everything he had ever written or acted in. Before coming to San Francisco, he had made a tour of the East with his Reformed Drunkard, which later he changed to Ten Nights In a Barroom, under which title it still remains as a classic of that period of the theatre. The Picayune, August 19, writes:

> "The increasing popularity of this beautiful little theatre, is decisive evidence both of the ability of the performers and of the taste of the community for rational entertainments in preference to the attractions of vulgar dissipations. The performance on Saturday evening drew a full house, and was excellently well sustained in each role.
>
> "The illustrations of the Drunkard's fall and wretchedness, we have never seen surpassed, in any place."

Much of the credit for the popularity of the theatre, it seems, must go to the supporting cast at the Museum. Discounting his over-enthusiasm for Senorita Llorente, the critic of the Picayune must have expressed the general feeling of pleasure at finally having a theatre in San Francisco that offered more than bare-back riders, acrobats and trained horses. In the August 22nd issue, he writes:

> "The performances at this popular place of amusement last night, were as attractive as usual. The pieces were 'Matrimony' and that popular old play entitled 'Perfection' in which Mlle. Duprez demonstrated the perfection to which they have arrived in the manufacture of cork legs in 'Ould Ireland.' Mr. Cook appeared in a new Irish dance, and 'kicked up his heels' to the tune of Rory O'More, and was encored--as he deserved to be.
>
> "The charming little Augustina Llorente--a dark-eyed maid of Castille--dark but comely--never looked more beautiful, and never danced with more grace than last night. But when at the conclusion, she fell into the arms of Senor

Aroyo, we could not help wishing that she were a dew drop, and---'we a butter-cup.'

"Last but not least, is Mrs. Burrill, who is the favorite of the establishment, and a most deservedly popular actress. She is always perfect in her part, and graceful in her acting. Her song--'The Maid of Monterey' was enthusiastically encored, and is, we learn, to be repeated this evening by particular request."

BENEFIT PERFORMANCES

A week later, on the 29th of August, the partner-managers set apart a night in the following week for a benefit for the relief fund for overland emigrants. Said the Picayune:

"We feel confident that such liberality on the part of these gentlemen who have recently lost their all, by fire, will be duly appreciated and not soon forgotten by this community."

On the same date, the Picayune carried a story of a benefit for Dr. Robinson to be held that night:

"There are very few in this community who know the difficulties with which Dr. Robinson has had to contend in getting his little Theatre in successful operation. The day after the late fire, in which he, with many others, lost their all, found him standing in Sacramento Street clad in a pair of duck trousers and red flannel shirt and with only 25 cents in his pocket, and owing $20 for board, which he had no means of paying. Like a true son of Maine, and possessing the true 'Yankee Spirit' and enterprise, he did not despair. With his own hands he shoveled out the sand for the foundation of the present Dramatic Museum, and he also handled every piece of timber in the frame of the building.

"He and his partner, Mr. Evrard, struggled on, with the assistance of a few kind friends, and completed the edifice, with only a debt over them of about $4,500. Up to yesterday, $4,000 of this amount had been paid, and they had the money on hand to pay the balance.

"Neither of the partners have drawn a dollar more from the concern than was absolutely necessary to pay their personal expenses, and this evening has been kindly set apart by his partner, for Dr. Robinson's benefit, to enable him to get a little funds to send to his family in the States. The writer of this has known Dr. Robinson for a long time, and has no hesitation in saying that there is not a more deserving man in California, or anywhere else...."

The Picayune of September 2 stated that the Dramatic Museum was filled to overflowing on the doctor's benefit night and that more than a hundred persons were turned away. On September 4, this periodical declared that the doctor had "Paid over the sum of nearly $200 into the relief fund."

SEIGE OF CHOLERA

These were, decidedly, busy days for the energetic doctor. On the 7th of September, he reciprocated his partner's kindness and gave Evrard a benefit in return for the one tendered him. On the 9th, he delivered a temperance address to a crowded house (and adds the Picayune) "with much force and eloquence."

Throughout September, the Dramatic Museum continued to draw full houses, and the doctor was able to acquire the services of traveling actors and to enlarge his repertoire. However, early in October, he became seriously ill with cholera and was forced to remain inactive from the theatre for more than two weeks. But under the management of James Evrard, the "Little Dramatic" continued on its prosperous way.

By the 16th of October, he had recovered sufficiently to be up and around and paid a visit to the office of the Picayune. His friends there wrote:

> "We were pleased to receive a visit yesterday from our friend, Dr. Robinson, who has been for some days past dangerously ill. He is improving rapidly, and his many friends may expect to greet him again shortly upon the stage. The Doctor is getting up a new piece which he proposes soon to present, in a style far superior to anything in the theatrical line that has yet been given in San Francisco."

It was not until the 23rd of October, however, that he recovered his health enough so as to be able to return to his post as chief manager. The Picayune of November 9 mentions a benefit which was tendered the Doctor on his recovery:

> "We are happy to learn that our talented and noble hearted friend, Dr. Robinson, has recovered from a late and severe attack of cholera, and that he will now resume the active part he has heretofore sustained in the performances at the Dramatic Museum. He has met with many reverses in the prosecution of his design, (the establishment of a respectable and creditable place of amusement) under which a less able and energetic man than he has shown himself to be, would have sunk. In view of these facts, we are gratified to be able to announce that the Doctor takes a benefit this evening at which time his numerous friends will have an opportunity of manifesting their appreciation of him."

However, while the house was well filled for the benefit performance, Dr. Robinson suffered a relapse and was too ill to appear.

During his early convalescence, the Doctor and his co-partner Evrard, decided to remodel the theatre since its success seemed well assured. The Daily Alta California of

November 4 wrote:

> "Evrard and Robinson's neat little place of amusement is doing a very good business. Very important alterations have been made in the audience part of the house, as well as the stage, which have relieved it from the cramped appearance it exhibited upon its first opening. It is now pretty and comfortable."

DRAMATIC MUSEUM'S BUSY PERIOD

In the past two months, the Dramatic Museum had taken on several new members and included several new plays in its repertoire. Mlle. Duprez made her first appearance on August 20, appearing in Matrimony and Perfection. Mrs. Mansfield made her debut on September 25 in Day After the Wedding supported by a Mr. Warren, a favorite amateur. In late September, they produced Charles II and The Used Up Man featuring Dr. Robinson's famous song of the same name. Hunting a Turtle and The Loan of a Lover were produced, the former for the first time in California, on September 30. On the 16th of October, three pieces were presented, The Widow, Turning the Tables and The Hole in the Wall, with Mr. Warren drawing a large crowd.

They again presented the San Francisco theatre audience with something new on November 4 in Naval Engagements (produced for the first time in California) and repeated Odd Fellow, the former eliciting great praise from the critics. On the night of Dr. Robinson's benefit, the theatre produced The Follies of a Night followed by an ambitious farce. Throughout the month of November, the phenomenal success of the Dramatic Museum continued.

NOVELTY PRESENTATIONS

Besides running through their popular plays, they presented innovations in the way of amusements such as the Scenic Representations of the Antediluvian World, a series of designs by the English artist, John Martin, K. L. This exhibition was "accompanied with appropriate music," according to the Picayune of November 16, "and by descriptive lectures from Dr. Robinson. The opinions of the public press in favor of these exhibitions are of the highest character, and the moral effect is likely to be of the happiest nature."

Another of the novelty presentations was their moving Panorama of Venice. This was a painting 18 feet in height and 2,956 long, costing $10,000. This gigantic scroll was probably the first "moving picture" presented in California.

It seems, however, that in spite of these innovations the Dramatic Museum was not only not making a fortune but the proprietors were struggling to barely break even. The Evening Picayune, January 2, 1851, reported a plan that Robinson and Evrard had in order to relieve themselves of some of their most pressing debts and to make certain alterations in their theatre:

> "The proprietors of the Dramatic Museum are compelled, by urgency of circumstances, to appeal to their numerous friends in San Francisco, to aid them in carrying out an object which they have in view, of much importance to themselves and the public, viz: that of liquidating all

their minor debts at once by disposing of a number of season tickets (for 6 months) at the unprecedented low price of $35.00. By the aid of their friends they hope to accomplish this and thereby be enabled to make their establishment still more attractive.

"Their previous efforts to meet the approbation of the public--the reverses they have met with, and the present popularity of their establishment--lead them to believe that it will be only necessary to appeal to their friends and the public, to have their wishes accomplished, and thereby enable them to cater hereafter with more ease to themselves and pleasure to their friends.

"P.S. Two persons can subscribe together for a ticket, which will entitle each to 3 months entrance."

COMPANY CRITICIZED

Whether this plan succeeded in its objective or not is unknown (no amount of research has disclosed any further information about its results) but, certainly, the Dramatic Museum continued on its hectic way. Plays were presented with but little rehearsal; at most with two or three days preparation, and there was much "ad libbing" on the stage. The Evening Picayune, January 4, 1851, criticized the Dramatic Museum company for this, stating that plays should not be repeated until the actors had made themselves better acquainted with their parts:

"Indeed, we advise all belonging to the Museum to 'stick close to the text.' It is seldom that a performer can, by extemporaneous remarks, improve the studied work of a successful author, but he may materially detract from the merits of the piece and seriously injure his own prospects by relying less upon the book than his own ready wit. The most successful artists are found apparently satisfied with representing characters as the author intended."

Later in January, James Evrard took a benefit. Mrs. Evrard, who had just arrived from New York where she had long been known as a pleasing actress, made her first appearance. Dr. Robinson, too, was tendered a benefit on the 20th of the month by his company and partner.

ROBINSON AS POLITICIAN

In the political field, the doctor was as busy as on the stage. Fortunately for him, in his position as alderman, he was fully able to protect the Dramatic Museum from within the legal machine. Early in March, when a group of California Street merchants presented a petition to the city council "praying that the board of aldermen would pass an ordinance prohibiting the extension of the Dramatic Museum which encroaches upon that street," the aldermen cheerfully referred it to the Street Commission, which as cheerfully no doubt, allowed it to die quietly within that body.

But Dr. Robinson was too good a showman to let slip opportunities like this. The audience at his theatre a few nights following would be treated to an uproarious song, full of jibes at his unfortunate political and business rivals. The popularity of Dr. Robinson was phenomenal.

During the mayorality campaign in April, the Independent People's Party nominated Dr. Robinson for mayor. Too fun-loving to take it seriously, he made a carnival of it; and although he lost the election, again, the audience at the Dramatic Museum was the winner.

Dr. Robinson had also finished a new song, "Hits at San Francisco" in which he made poetic digs at street contractors, fellow aldermen and other political enemies. He was busy in his position as alderman and derived much publicity in his joint role as politician and thespian. An amusing letter of his appeared in the Evening Picayune of February 13 in which he apologized for calling certain commissioners "thieves and robbers" and he was sorry that they were. "I felt justified in using the term. Respectfully yours, D. G. Robinson."

Another innovation that he introduced to the theatre was possibly the precursor of the modern "bank night." On February 14, 1851, at the conclusion of the evening's performances, an oil painting, "An Italian Landscape," was given away to the winner of a drawing of ticket stubs.

Back again to politics; on February 18, he presented a petition to the city council that the sidewalk in front of the Dramatic Museum be extended to twelve feet in width. On the 25th, he introduced an ordinance, which was passed unanimously, establishing a chain-gang for petty criminals.

On a Sunday afternoon in August, two criminals, Whittaker and McKenzie, were hanged by a Vigilance Committee in the rooms of the committee on Battery near California Street, after having been taken from the jail. The Evening

Picayune of August 25, said:

"They were swung from the threshhold! They died easily....when life was thought to be extinct Mr. S. Brannan was called forward and addressed the multitude in a most becoming manner;as also did Dr. Robinson and Stephen Payran...."

A NEW THEATRE

Dr. Robinson, at this time, was the co-manager of the New Adelphi Theatre, for, in May of 1851, San Francisco was again swept by fire, and the Dramatic Museum had been completely destroyed. Not the least daunted, Robinson immediately leased the New Adelphi Theatre on Dupont Avenue near Clay Street. This was the first French theatre in San Francisco, and Robinson, with Wiesenthall as co-manager, undertook the productions in English. His partner of the Dramatic Museum, James Evrard, had gone over to the new Jenny Lind to manage it for Tom Maguire. The Adelphi was a smaller theatre than the Jenny Lind but perfectly equipped.

For two months following the fire, it was the only theatre in San Francisco. The sprightly doctor secured the services of Mr. and Mrs. James Stark who had been driven out of Sacramento by a fire there in which they had lost not only all their belongings but also the chance to recoup their savings since all the theatres in Sacramento had also burned down. So Robinson signed up the Starks and offered the patrons of the Adelphi a repertoire of American stock plays. On August 22, the Starks were tendered a benefit at the Adelphi Says the Courier of this performance:

> "At the conclusion Mr. Stark was called out and made an admirable speech to the audience. When it became his duty to speak of the managers of the Adelphi, he became <u>choked for want of utterance</u>. We could appreciate his feelings, and no doubt Dr. Robinson and his associate, Mr. Wiesenthal, felt as the audience did."

During September, the Starks played two weeks and were followed by Harriet Carpenter and James Seymour in <u>Limerick Boy</u>. In October, however, Dr. Robinson resigned as manager of the New Adelphi. Bigger plans were afoot, for in the meantime, Tom Maguire had opened his Jenny Lind III. In sheer size and ornateness, it far eclipsed the Adelphi and the best that Robinson had been able to do in competition was to anticipate <u>All that Glitters is not Gold</u>," the Jenny Lind's initial opus, at the Adelphi.

NEW BUILDING ERECTED

But Dr. Robinson had not really been caught flat-footed. A new theatre building, under his direction, was rapidly nearing completion. On the 16th of September, the <u>Evening Picayune</u> reported:

> "Having observed in the morning papers a notice of the laying of the cornerstone of a new theatre yesterday morning, we started down Sansome Street at about 11 o'clock today to take a look at the ground. What was our surprise to find that one story of the building was already built, the sleepers laid, and the flooring of the pit and stage going down as fast as hammers could fall, and nails be driven.
>
> "We never remember, in all our experiences of California building, to have seen anything which could begin to compare with this. The idea of a brick building of one hundred and twenty feet

in length and fifty-five in breadth, rising at a
rate of a story a day, reminds us of the palace
of Aladdin, a little more strongly than anything
we have ever heard of.

"If the Dr. gets on at the same rate much longer
we will expect to see a couple of thousand persons listening to one of his songs in the new
building on the evening of the day after tomor-
row."

However, the new theatre was a substantial building and could not be so rapidly constructed. Four days after the above article appeared, the Picayune said:

"The edifice now going up for Messrs. Robinson
and Wiesenthall is going ahead very rapidly under the management of A. P. Petit, architect,
and J. H. Atkinson, mason. Indeed, we have
scarcely ever seen so great speed combined with
finish and substantiality displayed in the erection of a building. The secret is the superin-
tendence of able men and the employment of good
mechanics.

"The building is 120 feet deep with a 55 foot
front which will soon be increased in the amount
of 40 feet. The cornerstone was laid on Monday
last and already the wall is up all around to a
height of 18 feet and the floor of the pit, the
first tier of boxes, and the stage are laid. The
foundation is laid on heavy wooden timbers, and
commences 3 feet in thickness; it gradually tap-
ers to 20 inches which will be the thickness of
the main walls of the building.

"Stout iron anchors are to be set in the walls,
which will render them amply safe. The theatre
will be 35 feet high and will be completed within 25 days."

Dr. Robinson and Wiesenthall, the partners of the New Adelphi, were co-proprietors of the new American Theatre, and James Stark was installed as manager and lessee of the house.

THEATRICAL COMPETITION

The managerial competition between the genial doctor and Maguire for the theatrical supremacy of San Francisco was now well under way. While the American was under construction, rumors, reported emanating from Maguire's friends, were current that the new theatre building was unsafe. It was one of the first to be constructed on beach-water property of the newly filled-in bay, on Sansome between Sacramento and California Streets. The Courier of October 1, says:

> "This is a grand country for rumors. A ridiculous report was currently circulated about town yesterday that the building now in course of construction on Sansome Street by Messrs. Robinson and Wiesenthall, was being constructed in a careless and insecure manner....We....are perfectly satisfied that there exists not the slightest cause for apprehension regarding the safety of the structure...The walls are so interlocked and braced with iron that even should the building settle several feet, there will be no cause to apprehend injury to the walls. The proscenium walls are very heavy and constructed of brick and consequently contribute a large amount of support to the main walls....In justice to Messrs. Robinson and Wiesenthall, who have spared no exertion and have expended their whole combined capital in the erection of this building, it is to be hoped that an idle report got up by some mischief-loving person will not have the least effect upon the patrons of their theatre."

AMERICAN THEATRE OPENS

In spite of these ill-founded rumors, the opening night of the American Theatre was a great success. The walls did sink two inches but no damage other than this was noted. The initial play was Armand; or, The Peer and the Peasant, by

Anna Cora Mowatt. James Stark took the title role of Armand, supported by the Chapman family. Mrs. Stark gave the opening address which had been written in verse by Dr. Robinson. The <u>Courier</u> said:

> "This bijou of a theatre was opened last evning to the perfect delight of a brilliant and enthusiastic assemblage of the drama....The front circle glittered with a galaxy of fashion and beauty."

In the theatre seating only 2,000, two thousand six hundred and thirty-five tickets were sold in addition to standing room. The price of two dollars tops and fifty cents for galleries was also an innovation for that period, previous prices being from $3 to $5 tops and $1 for galleries. Accordingly, the Jenny Lind later was forced to cut prices.

There were many in the audience who realized that some of the new ventures were overly ambitious, that parts were over-acted and productions were put together with more enthusiasm than art, but the genial spirit of Dr. Robinson called forth all the sense of humor and warmth in the audience and the theatre prospered accordingly.

Shouts of "Tell us a story, tell us a story" would always call the sprightly little doctor before the curtain between acts where he interspersed his impersonations with local songs. In spite of stiff competition from Maguire of the Jenny Lind III, the American's 2,000 seats were always in demand. Stars of the theatrical world were used as pawns in the managerial rivalry; the Doctor having in his cast the

Starks, the Chapman family, Emily Coad and the Lee family to vie with the Booths that Maguire had under his wing. But Dr. Robinson eventually came to grief through his young son, Charles....

ROBINSON - STARK FEUD

The Starks were appearing in a melodrama (the type of play which, with their Shakespearean interpretations, had made them famous) called The Stranger. Little Charles had a walk-on bit with one short speech opposite Mrs. Stark. On the night of October 31, so the story goes, austere Mrs. Robinson had brought Charles down from their home on Telegraph Hill in time for his appearance on the stage. He was tired and sleepy and when his cue was given, he appeared on the stage, dressed in a red suit, only to curse Mrs. Stark in a language no doubt patterned after that of his father, Dr. Robinson. There is no proof that it was learned for this purpose although the Starks accused the Robinsons of this and never believed otherwise. From then on, The Robinson-Stark feud was on.

When Robinson planned Othello as the next major production of the American Theatre with Stark and Thorne as the principal characters, disagreement arose as to who should play Iago and who the title role. The Alta California of November 28 says:

> "Owing to some professional misunderstanding between Messrs. Stark and Thorne, the play of

> 'Othello,' which was put upon the bills, was not played, instead of which, the comedy 'Honey Moon' was performed.'"

In the interim, Stark must have been approached by the Jenny Lind management for, on November 27, a benefit was performed there for Stark with himself as King Lear. Stark was no longer "choked with lack of utterance" in gratitude to Dr. Robinson.

On December 15, the American Theatre produced Mazeppa with C. R. Thorne in the starring role. In the afterpiece of the double-feature show, Dr. Robinson made a hit as Charles Freeheart in The Reformed Drunkard but it was, in general, a losing fight for theatrical supremacy against Tom Maguire.

By Christmas of that year, Robinson had assumed full control of the American Theatre. Wiesenthall was no longer connected with the enterprise. With the reduction of the Jenny Lind prices (an innovation set by Dr. Robinson which boomeranged) on February 9, Robinson was finally forced to admit defeat. Ten days later, he gave a final performance featuring himself, at the conclusion of which, his son Charles, indirectly the cause of his decline, dressed in the memorable red suit, sang "Nary a Red, Nary a Red." Following the performance, Robinson entertained friends and fellow workers of the American Theatre at a champagne dinner at his Telegraph Hill home.

TELEGRAPH HILL HOME

He remained on the outskirts of the theatrical profession even while taking no active part in the entertainment world. His home at 9 Calhoun Place was always popular with the members of his profession.

Even as late as 1917, the fame of his home still lived, for the _Bulletin_ of January 27 carried a story by Pauline Jacobson illustrated with a photograph of the house. A caption over the photo read "Historic house where the Booths spent pleasant hours." The story continued:

> "The home of Dr. 'Yankee' Robinson still stands at No. 9 Calhoun Street, on Telegraph Hill. In the fifties it was a rendezvous for many of the talented men, among them the great tragedian, Edwin Booth, who found inspiration in the virile life of the California pioneers.
>
> "Dr. Robinson's house still stands as the rise of the ground put it beyond the flames of 1906. It still bears the pioneer numbering, crudely painted, in white 'No. 9' on the facade of the gateway. It is a two story gabled frame house with a garden and trees--a palatial home for that period when lumber was high and labor even more so. The house fronts the sea, in command of a most magnificent sweep of the bay, to three points of the compass.
>
> "And Charles Robinson, the artist, son of Dr. Robinson, tells me that the house of 'June' Booth was of much the same order. They each bought a fifty-vara* lot and each built a home of much the same style and dimensions. The Booth home has been but recently torn down to make way for an imposing modern structure in the rear of the lot. The front of both lots has been undermined, and Sansome Street at this point has entirely disappeared, owing to the crumbling away of the hill."

---

*Vara- Spanish yard; equivalent to 33.5 inches.

Besides the Booths, his other neighbors included Mrs. Crabtree and her small daughter Lotta, Sophie Edwin, and Mrs. Stark. Mrs. Judah, the Grand Old Woman of the California stage, was always a welcome guest at his home. Lola Montez also stayed with Dr. Robinson on her arrival in San Francisco.

ROBINSON - MAGUIRE RECONCILIATION

While the genial doctor's prestige was declining, Maguire's fortunes had been more favorable. With young Junius Booth as manager, and featuring the Chapmans, the San Francisco Theatre was now the premier theatre in the city after which it was named. Maguire was too good a showman to allow any personal differences in the past to keep such an attraction as Doc Robinson off his stage. The <u>Golden Era</u>, January 2, 1853, reported and predicted:

> "The company here (the San Francisco Theatre) has recently had an acquisition in the person of the far-famed Dr. Robinson. He will sing a new and popular song.....
>
> "This must render the San Francisco Hall under the management of Chapman and Booth one of the most popular places of amusements in the city."

And so it proved.

Maguire was a clever manager -- and at heart a gentleman. Knowing that Robinson would turn down an offer of a mere job, he, Maguire, had given Robinson a chance to save face. The approach was this: Signor Tremendous of the company had left unexpectedly for New York, leaving an open spot in the cast which had to be filled; would Dr. Robinson as an old trouper, knowing that "the show must go on," fill in that spot to help Maguire and the cast? Dr. Robinson would -- and did.

He opened on the first Wednesday in January and, reported the Golden Era, presented

> "...a 'bran new' song of some lenth, but being somewhat out of voice, he could get through with only a portion of it--forty-six verses. The Doctor, however, made a hit on this, as he has on all occasions.
>
> "We understand that the Doctor would not have accepted the engagement had it not been for the void created by the departure of Signor Tremendous....The Doctor certainly deserves great credit for thus timely jumping into the breach!"

On January 16, he appeared in the comedy of All Is Not Gold That Glitters much to the surprise of the Golden Era critic who reported with some amazement that

> "...The Doctor, for once in his life, cast aside the role of comicality and gave us a new proof of his versatility as Jasper Plum."

But the exuberant Doctor was not happy appearing in plays and reading lines that someone else had written. He insisted on appearing only between the curtains or as an afterpiece with his own songs, and Maguire acquiesced. The Golden Era, February 6, 1853, mentioned one of the benefit performances for Dr. Robinson at which he presented a new song:

> "On Monday night the inimitable Dr. took what he humorously called one of his farewell benefits on which occasion he appeared in a new song which was received with much laughter at the expense of our 'city fathers'."

The San Francisco Hall became one of the most

vigorous theatres of the nation. Offering a continually changing program of Shakespeare to burlesque, concerts to acrobatics, to which Dr. Robinson added as an afterpiece his now perennial favorites, the "Old Umbrella," "Random Rhymes," and other original songs, the San Francisco Hall night after night hung out S. R. O. (standing room only) signs....

COMING OF LOLA MONTEZ

Then Lola Montez came to San Francisco, preceded by a glamourous and intriguing story of her past she became an attraction by herself which eclipsed the box-office appeal of the joint stars of the San Francisco Hall. In a spirit of professional rivalry, the cast of the San Francisco Hall resented the adulation heaped upon this exotic dancer and mime appearing at the American Theatre.

From the cast at the San Francisco Theatre, Dr. Robinson and Caroline Chapman attended a performance of Maritana in which Lola took three parts. These two remorseless satirists went out to supper after the play and collaborated on a burlesque which was quickly whipped into shape and produced the next night at their theatre. Caroline Chapman went Lola four better by taking seven parts in the uproarious skit, The Actress of All Work.

Lola then presented an autobiographical play dealing with her adventures in Europe. Dr. Robinson and Caroline Chapman countered with Lola Montez in Bavaria a broad burlesque and a lively extravaganza.

Now Lola's <u>piece de resistance</u> was her famous Spider Dance in which she impersonated in dance form, a woman shaking spiders off her dress. Finally, Dr. Robinson finished the script for a three-act burlesque called <u>Who's Got The Countess</u> in which every innuendo-tinted rumor of Lola's past was exaggerated into high relief, and in which the subtle and veiled indelicacies of her spider dance were turned into the bold sexy gyrations of a strumpet under the suggestive title of "Spy-dear."

ORIGINAL MONTEZ BURLESQUE

Caroline Chapman accepted the part with zest. A thin, awkward showboat product but a daring and accomplished comedienne, she made up in vivacity and personality all that she lacked in grace and beauty. Whether her eagerness to burlesque the beauty and grace of Lola was a desire to belittle or whether she appreciated the comedy value of the part is problematical.

However, the play was a great success, the <u>Golden Era</u> of June 26 congratulating Dr. Robinson

> "upon producing the first successful original piece in California..."

but feeling that the Spider or "Spy-dear" Dance was laid on "a <u>leetle</u> too thick."

The Herald, championing Lola, was much more indignant. It described the piece as

> "...an exceedingly coarse and vulgar attack upon one who, whatever her faults and foibles may

have been, has proved herself a noble-hearted and generous woman...a vulgar representation of her manners and behavior, a ridiculous caricature of her person and a coarse exaggeration of her peculiarities."

A more critical review is that which appeared in the *Daily Alta California*:

"A new local burlesque and extravaganza has been played at the San Francisco Theatre during the past week, written by Dr. Robinson. Crowds of persons have been to see it, and it has been the gossip of the theatre-going public since it was put on the stage. It is a hit at the engagement and appearance among us of a celebrated personage, and contains a few clever allusions. The clever merit consists in the admirable personation of Mr. and Miss Chapman of a prominent theatrical gentleman and the notable in question. The plot of the piece--if it may be called a plot--is very miserably arranged and the dialogue lacking in wit, point, appropriateness and even common sense, and is, to drown all, bunglingly arranged in bad rhyme. There are one or two very happy lines, however, and ludicrous surprises, which together with the dance by Mr. Chapman ... and Miss Caroline's imitations before mentioned, redeem the piece and have even made it popular. The theatre has been crowded every night, and the burlesque received shouts of laughter."

A few days later, the same critic, still unfavorably disposed to the burlesque but immensely entertained by Dr. Robinson, commented on the popularity of the theatre:

"There was a crowd last night at the San Francisco Theatre. A new song by Dr. Robinson brought down the house repeatedly, being as full of local hits as it was destitute of poetry. It was the most entertaining part of the evening's performances, however, and we propose to take a little credit to ourselves, for it would seem our criticisms of the burlesque 'Who's Got the Countess?' drew it out. The song was well put, though we must adhere to our opinion that the play is without reason and would be better without rhyme."

Lola could not understand this seemingly derogatory attack on her. She had stayed with the Robinsons on her arrival in San Francisco and Mrs. Robinson, disapproving as she was of the theatre, had taken kindly to Lola and had even helped her sew the rubber spiders on Lola's dancing costume. Lola asked Dr. Robinson for an explanation of this satire on her and was answered by a theatrical paraphrasing of an old bromide: "Imitation is the sincerest form of flattery."

Nevertheless, the piece proved a splendid drawing card for several weeks and was subsequently presented as an afterpiece on changing bills. Eventually, the farce included the whole cast of the American Theatre, not forgetting the prompter -- a daring dig at Lola's reputed inability to learn her lines. While there is no evidence to bear out the contention of Dr. Robinson and Caroline Chapman that they were instrumental in driving Lola off the boards, Lola did announce her withdrawal from the stage. A few weeks later, she married a San Franciscan.

MANAGES SUE ROBINSON

The story of Dr. Robinson's success in San Francisco began filtering its way back East, and like a lodestone, it drew the eyes and ambitions of the large Robinson family towards the new country. Among those who finally came out to San Francisco was Sue Robinson, a child at that time of about four or five.

Though they bore the same surname Dr. Robinson and Sue were not related, according to the doctor's granddaughter, Lillian. However, Sue, on her arrival in San Francisco lived with Dr. Robinson in the New England house he had built among the dramatic colony then flourishing on Telegraph Hill. The doctor quickly discerned in this young girl a certain aptitude for the stage. After coaching her and putting her through a short period of training, he decided to capitalize on the popularity of child stars in the outer regions.

Coincidentally, shortly after the departure of Lola Montez to Australia with her husband, the American Theatre was forced to close for a time. The cast of the San Francisco decided to take advantage of this period of inactivity in the competitive theatrical whirl of the city and to make tours through the mining regions. The Chapmans left first. Later, Dr. Robinson and his young protege, Sue Robinson, also departed for the mines.

After a wholly satisfactory and remunerative tour of Grass Valley, Nevada City and other mining towns, the Robinsons returned to San Francisco.

NEW AND ORIGINAL BURLESQUE

In late August, Dr. Robinson, perhaps encouraged by the success of his Montez burlesque and financially replenished by his tour, presented at the San Francisco Theatre his new and original burlesque, California -- Past, Present and Future. Intended originally as an historical panorama, it deeply impressed the critics of that time. The Golden Era, August 28 wrote:

> "Dr. Robinson, who has shown himself to be an author as well as an actor, has succeeded in producing upon the boards of the San Francisco Theatre, a play which, if we are not mistaken, will have a more successful run than anything ever brought out in California. The title,'California--Past, Present and Future' is the most appropriate that could have been selected while the plot and language carry with them much that is pleasing to those who have witnessed the vicissitudes of life in California."

He had intended this to be an historical panorama in the grand style, and the play gained fame and special lustre later when Captain Sutter was added to the cast to impersonate himself. The Golden Era continued:

> "The piece improves on each presentation, and if properly cared for by those engaged in its performance, we predict for the San Francisco Theatre, a succession of the most crowded audiences ever congregated in a San Francisco theatre."

But the early training under the great Barnum, plus the demands of the public, quickly erased the serious aspects of the play. The pageant became more and more humorous and Dr. Robinson was busy continually padding it with topical allusions and extraneous skits. He added a burlesque on the subject of woman's rights; he wrote in a part about a boy who had accidentally gone up in a balloon and had it floated over the bay.

Finally, Dr. Robinson was replaced at the San Francisco Theatre by a minstrel troupe. But he would never give up his original plan for his dramatic pageant; he clung tenaciously to his desire to produce it seriously. It became the one great wish of his life, but he knew that it could never be revived in San Francisco -- it had to be taken elsewhere.

CAREER ABRUPTLY ENDED

On the 17th of June, 1856 he was tendered a farewell benefit at the Union Theatre, the proceeds of which were to send him East where he intended to produce <u>California -- Past, Present and Future</u> on the legitimate stage. He sailed for the Atlantic states on the 20th of the month....But he fell ill enroute of ship's fever and died at Mobile, Alabama. Dr. Robinson's dramatic historical pageant was destined never to be produced.

The passing of Dr. Robinson broke the one link in the chain which had bound San Francisco's theatrical adolescence to the infant days of its pioneer stage. The "Roaring Forties" old-timers mourned the loss of the man who had given San Francisco its robust, boisterous, rough and broad humor on the stage when the theatre was young.

LEAVES VIVID MEMORIES

Walter Leman reminisces in his <u>Memories of an Old Actor</u> and remembers Dr. Robinson as

> "...one of the early comers to the land of gold. He had played in the mining regions of Oregon and California and the lavish favors of fortune had been followed by her frowns so often that he had become alike indifferent to frown or smile...."
>
> "I do not think that Dr. Robinson had ever received anything like theatrical training...but he was 'up' in everything and some parts he played well...."

Even as late as 1916, he was still a vivid figure in the memories of early San Franciscans. Pauline Jacobson, in her article titled "Classics Echo in Toasts of the Argonauts," the San Francisco Bulletin, April 15, 1916, in which she wrote about early days on Montgomery Street, said:

> "Here in these chairs sat great lawyers and orators, who, when they had an address to make, came here to talk it over and try it out with a few friends. For the saloon was a great forum and theatre as well. Here the poet recited his verse, the actor tried his lines, the orator his speech. Nor did men in those days, when they had a speech to make, go to the encyclopedia, as men do today. Everybody knew the classics; his Homer, his Virgil and his Shakespeare.
>
> "And here sat Dr. Robinson--Yankee Robinson called--the father of Charles Dorman Robinson, dean of the artists, and the only one today who was present when California was admitted into the Union. Dr. Robinson founded the first theatre. He was a poet as well. His 'Random Rhymes,' satirizing the municipal officers, and which were given on his own stage, gained him such great popularity that he was made alderman and was named as the most popular candidate for Mayor."

Dr. Robinson left behind him a stage that was so virile that subsequent weak casts, theatrical squabblings and poor management could not kill it. The tradition of the lusty theatre and the title of "Dr." still remain as nostalgic memorabilia of the colorful, exciting, virile and passionate theatre and actors of Forty-Nine.

DAVID G. (YANKEE) ROBINSON
ADDENDA

Miss Lillian M. Robinson, granddaughter of the pioneer showman, who lives in San Rafael, graciously granted this project a personal interview. As a result much information hitherto unavailable in spite of indefatigable research was disclosed; much that was confused about Dr. Robinson's early years has been straightened out; and much that had been accepted as true has been found wanting.

Charles Dorman Robinson, only child of Dr. Robinson and father of Lillian, was an eminent personality in his own right, being one of California's famed painters. Before his death he gathered together much material about his father, made copious notes, all with the intention of writing when he found the leisure an accurate account of his and his father's lives. He died before this plan reached more than the material-gathering stage. However, Miss Robinson had several books dealing with early California in which her father had made voluminous marginal notes, pointing out the inaccuracies of the respective authors. From Miss Robinson this project secured the facts concerning the doctor's early life and presents them here for the first time in print.

Dr. Robinson's wife and young son, Charles Dorman, then only two or three years old, came to San Francisco from Monmouth, Maine, after the doctor had his pharmacy so well started that there would be no danger that the family would find itself economically stranded in this new and wild country. Mrs. Robinson became an actress, said her granddaughter, and a very good one although she always detested the stage (page 101). It was not long before she told her husband that she "was through with the stage" but she did nothing to hinder him from his many theatrical activities. "In fact," Lillian Robinson reports, "she was such an immaculate housekeeper and cooked so excellently that her home was continually filled with actors and actresses, many of whom remained for long periods of time." (pages 94, 95, 96)

Although a fund of research material available to the project shows that Dr. Robinson managed the child actress, Sue Robinson, nothing ever indicated that she was related to the doctor (pages 101, 102). Lillian Robinson states emphatically that neither Sue nor Fayette Lodawick "Yankee" Robinson* were relatives. "In fact," she said, "this is the first I've ever heard of them."

Dr. Robinson's death in Mobile, Alabama, in 1856

---

* Fayette Lodawick Robinson, also called "Yankee" as was Dr. Robinson, had other points of similarity which often confused chroniclers of early theatrical history. Fayette was a showman of much the same type as David, playing Yankee parts, exhibiting Scriptural paintings which he transported from town to town in a one-horse wagon, and erecting a tent at Rock Island, Illinois, which he called the "Robinson Athenaeum" where he played The Drunkard and other similar pieces. T. Allston Brown in his History of the American Stage (Dick and Fitzgerald, New York, 1870) states that Fayette was "a direct lineal descendant of Dr. Robinson, the eminent divine, who came to this country in the Mayflower." (see page 73 in monograph) But Fayette Lodawick Robinson was born near Avon Mineral Springs, Livingston County, New York, May 2, 1818.

was tragic (page 105). An epidemic of yellow fever was sweeping the seaports of the Southern states. Passengers and crew on the ship, on which Dr. Robinson was carrying his high hopes to the east, were afflicted. Dr. Robinson was not exempt from the great plague. When he died in Mobile, deaths were so numerous that bodies were immediately buried and destroyed in quicklime graves and no records were kept of the burial place. Only the briefest indentification records were kept.

For months Mrs. Robinson and Charles waited in San Francisco for word from the far-distant husband and father. The son became bitter towards his father and always resented the manner in which his father had left the family in San Francisco while he went east to try his luck. Finally word trickled back to the Pacific Coast of Dr. Robinson's death. Charles and his mother sold their Telegraph Hill home at 9 Calhoun Place (page 95) and in about 1860 or 1862 settled in Vermont.

Subsequently, said Lillian Robinson, it was found that Dr. Robinson had taken his manuscripts of plays, among them The Reformed Drunkard, with him. These were stolen from his belongings on his death and The Reformed Drunkard appeared later in Atlantic cities as a re-vamped play called Ten Nights in a Bar-Room (see pages 78, 79 in monograph).

For the play California--Past, Present and Future which was the piece de resistance that he was taking east, he had a backdrop showing a bridge across San Francisco Bay (pages 103, 104). His may have been the original idea for the present San Francisco-Oakland Bay Bridge.

According to Miss Robinson, her father, Charles Dorman Robinson, felt quite bitter toward Dr. Robinson for his seeming desertion of his family, but, on the other hand, was far more wrathful with writers of books of that period in San Francisco. His caustic marginalia in which he defends his father from what he thought to be ridicule shows that he was not so much incensed at his father as at the fact that his father's acts which seemingly lacked dignity should be historically made public.

In one of his annotations, it is stated that Dr. Robinson built the Adelphi Theatre (page 88). No evidence has been uncovered other than to show that Dr. Robinson and Wiesenthall leased this French Theatre to give the English productions there.

"It is all false," says Charles in referring to the story of the early days of the Dramatic Museum and Dr. Robinson's popularity (pages 75, 76, 77). In this opinion, he runs counter to Constance Rourke's <u>Troupers of the Gold Coast</u>, Catherine Coffin Phillips' <u>Portsmouth Plaza, The Cradle of San Francisco</u>, and to contemporary newspaper accounts.

"False," notes Charles tersely about the champagne dinner for the American Theatre company and crew (page 94) at his Telegraph Hill home after the doctor was forced to give up the theatre. But what else would the genial, friendly Dr. Robinson have done -- gone off by himself to mope? He remained strictly in character in this act of good fellowship.

The Doc was what a public figure of great popularity and with hosts of friends in those days had to be: genial, warm-hearted, never standing on dignity, quick-witted and ready in repartee, and with the daring and initiative of a pioneer. It was Dr. Robinson and men like him that built the theatre in San Francisco. This city owes much to him and will always revere him for what he was, not for posthumous dignity which makes a man a mere bronze statue sitting forgotten in some nook of the city.

- - - - -

DR. DAVID G. (YANKEE) ROBINSON

Representative parts taken by Dr. Robinson

Date	Role	Play
1850	Seth Slopes	Seeing the Elephant
	Hezekiah Pickerall	Yankee stories and songs
	Charles	The Jew and the Doctor
1851	Charles Freeheart	The Reformed Drunkard
	Captain Copp	Charles II or Merry Monarch
1853	Jasper Plum	All is Not Gold That Glitters

DR. DAVID G. (YANKEE) ROBINSON

Theatres Associated With Dr. Robinson

Date	Name	Position
1849	Small audience hall name unknown	Builder, manager
1850	Dramatic Museum	Builder, co-manager with James Evrard
1851	New Adelphi	Builder, co-manager with Wiesenthall
1852	American	Builder, manager

BIBLIOGRAPHY OF DR. ROBINSON'S WORKS

Name	Classification
The Old Umbrella	Song and pantomime act
Used Up Miner	Ballad
Seeing the Elephant (adapted)	Musical comedy
The Victim	Melodrama
Reformed Drunkard (later renamed Ten Nights in a Bar Room)	"
Used Up Man	Musical comedy
Hamlet	Burlesque
Nary a Red, Nary a Red	Song
Random Rhymes	"
Actress of All Work	Burlesque
Lola Montez in Bavaria	"
Who's Got the Countess?	"
California--Past, Present and Future	"
Used Up Alderman	Song
Yellow Dwarf	Burlesque
Ins and Outs or Devil at the Crossroads	"
Wanted--1000 Milliners	"
Coarse-haired Brothers	"
Buy It, Dear; It's Made of Cashmere	"
Did You Ever send Your Wife to San Jose?	"
Woman's Rights, or Sleep of 100 Years	"

DR. DAVID G. (YANKEE) ROBINSON
BIBLIOGRAPHY

Foster, Lois M. *Annals of the San Francisco Stage*
    (Mss. unpub., Federal Theatre, San Francisco, 1937)

Leavitt, M. B. *Fifty Years in Theatrical Management*
    (Broadway Publishing Co., New York, N.Y., 1912)

Leman, Walter M. *Memories of an Old Actor*
    (A. Roman Co., San Francisco, 1886)

Lloyd, Benjamin Estelle. *Lights and Shades in San Francisco*
    (A. L. Bancroft and Co., San Francisco, 1876)

Rourke, Constance. *Troupers of the Gold Coast*
    (Harcourt, Brace and Co., New York, N.Y. 1928)

Phillips, Catherine Coffin. *Portsmouth Plaza*
    (John Henry Nash, San Francisco, 1932)

NEWSPAPERS AND PERIODICALS

The Bulletin: April 15, 1916; Jan. 27, Feb. 3, 1917.

Daily Evening Bulletin: June 17, 1856.

Daily Alta California: June 15; Sept. 2; Nov. 4, 1850.

Golden Era: Jan. 2, 3, 9; June 26; Aug. 29, 1853; June 17, 1856.

Evening Picayune: Aug. 7, 9, 13, 16, 19, 20, 22, 29; Sept. 2, 4, 7, 9, 13, 25, 30; Oct. 14, 16, 23; Nov. 4, 6, 7, 9, 11, 15, 16, 17, 20, 25; Dec. 4, 5, 10, 11, 31, 1850; Jan. 2, 4, 9, 10, 20; Feb. 4, 12, 13, 14, 18, 25; Mar. 4; April 11, 12, 16, 19, 22; Aug. 2, 5, 9, 15, 19, 25, 29, 30; Sept. 16, 20, 1851.

TABLE OF CONTENTS

MICHAEL M. LEAVITT -- (1843 - 1935)

	PAGES
Actor-Manager and Father of Vaudeville	109-142
Genesis of Vaudeville	110
Moppet Impresario and Actor	112
A Start in Earnest	113
Branching out -- on Tour	116
A Series of Adventures	119
En Route to the West	123
Variety, Burlesque and Vaudeville	125
Established in San Francisco	127
Success and Affluence	130
Retires from San Francisco after 20 years	136
Some of his Business Associates	140
Booking Managers who Worked for Leavitt	140
Performers and Companies Managed by Leavitt	141-143
Theatres Managed or Leased by Leavitt	143
Press Agents who Worked for Leavitt	144
Bibliography	145
Newspapers and Periodicals	145

MICHAEL B. LEAVITT
1843 - 1935

PHOTO FROM "FIFTY YEARS OF THEATRICAL MANAGEMENT"

MICHAEL B. LEAVITT

Actor-Manager and Father of Vaudeville

The Golden Age of the theatre in San Francisco was the period in which the resident manager was in his hey-day. And in those days the manager rolled up his sleeves and took care of every detail of all productions at his theatre, for, during that period, the manager was everything -- booking agent, press agent, stage manager, theatre manager, director and, usually in addition, the star of the company.

In the theatres devoted to the production of legitimate drama, this worked little hardship. Actors, depending on their position in the sock and buskin hierarchy,* were familiar with the roles in their respective category in the thirty or more standard plays included in every legitimate theatre repertoire. The theatre's stock company was complete from star down to the second comedian and spear-bearer. The termination of a play's run was not the end of the season -- the season was long and the company ran through its full

---

*See monograph on John McCullough

repertoire before the dramatic season came to a close.

But then came the days when the public tired of the old stand-bys. Shakespeare was good drama but it palled on the surfeited public; stock companys were composed of good actors but even good actors, the audience discovered, invariably had the same faces and the same voices regardless of roles essayed. Burlesques, variety shows, minstrels, circuses, magicians, song and dance teams, acrobats, dancers and dialect comedians -- all used previously as light after-pieces-- now became the headliners and received top billing.

GENESIS OF VAUDEVILLE

Theatre managers, then, found it necessary to devote their full time purely to business, managerial and booking agent duties. Vaudeville, as we know it today; circuits, in their present form, and syndicates, in all their ramification, were all unknown. Thus, arose an immediate problem. Each theatre manager had to be his own talent scout. He found that, in order to be able to continually offer his patrons a varied and interesting program, he necessarily had to go into the field and sign up performing troupes in his vicinity, pay their fare to his theatre, arrange playing dates and publicity; and if their acts were not long enough to make up a complete bill, an additional troupe was required, entailing a multiplicity of work and confusion.

The obvious answer -- the present form of vaudeville circuit with a central booking office -- was slow in coming.

That it did come, however, was due largely to the business acumen of one man who died a millionaire as a result of his perspicacity.

Mr. M.B.Leavitt, the founder of the theatrical circuit and the first agent to have a New York home office for booking Pacific Coast tours, was born in Posen, West Prussia on June 25, 1843 and was brought to this country when a little over a year old by his parents. They made their first home in Boston, Massachusetts, later moving to Bangor, Maine, and again to Hartford, Connecticut. To this continual traveling in his early days, he attributes the "spirit of adventure which has impelled me to visit all parts of the world."*

> "This first manifested itself (he continues) when I was about five years of age, and strayed away from home to run to a fire like older persons in the neighborhood. A guardian of the peace picked me up and led me to a house on Sudbury Street, Boston, where there was a temporary lodging for lost youngsters. The place was full at the time, and I had to sleep with one of the attendants, while the town crier (Sam Edwards by name), ringing a large bell, walked through the streets, shouting 'Child lost!' and giving descriptions of those picked up. In a day or two my father came, and carried me home on his shoulders and earnestly placed me across his knee. I remember this latter part of the proceedings more vividly than all the rest."

When Leavitt was seven years old he matriculated at the Tyler Street School, Boston, where he was a prize pupil, being fond of books and able to assimilate the lessons readily. As one of the talented pupils, he was chosen to recite

---

*M.B.Leavitt, <u>Fifty Years of Theatrical Management</u>, p.1

for the edification of Louis Hossuth when the "Magyar Patriot" visited the school one day. The piece selected for reading was <u>Bingen on the Rhine</u>, and at its conclusion the honor guest patted Leavitt on the head and complimented him.

<u>MOPPET IMPRESARIO AND ACTOR</u>

In 1852, when Leavitt was nine years old, the family moved to Bangor. Here he continued his schooling; and it was here where he began to develop tendencies toward the stage. He organized a minstrel and drama corps among his friends and many performances were given -- most of them creditable. He fitted up a miniature theatre in the barn with curtains, footlights, and some scenery -- all of which he loaned, at one time or another, to visiting touring troupes.

The reputation he built up in this self-initiated stage gave him the entrée to the various troupes which came to town. He became familiar with the managers and constituted himself a committee of one to carry the champagne baskets in which the wardrobe was transported. When the Wm. B. English company played Bangor, (and it was the custom in those days to pick a local friend of the theatre manager to fill in minor child roles rather than carry a youngster along with them on the road), Leavitt was picked as the logical one to fill this role in the cast. He made his stage debut as the child in <u>The Stranger</u> and as the young Duke of York in <u>Richard III</u>.

When Andrew Macallister, "The Great Macallister," brought his magical entertainments to Bangor, Leavitt acted as his assistant, rehearsing such feats as being shot out of a cannon and being run through with swords while inside a basket. His father being engaged in mercantile pursuits which occasionally necessitated his going to New York, took Leavitt on one of these trips. Here he saw the first appearance in America of the great French actress, Mme. Rachel, at the Metropolitan Theatre. At this time he was twelve years old.

What delighted Leavitt most on his stay in the great metropolis was his visit to Barnum's Museum at the corner of Broadway and Ann Streets. Barnum was presenting an excellent stock company, giving two performances a day in "The Lecture Room" of the museum. This visit to New York crystallized Leavitt's desire to make the stage his career.

A START IN EARNEST

At the age of thirteen, after making up his mind to pursue a theatrical career, he began considering what branch of the profession he would follow. He had already developed a fair singing voice, and had learned to play the piano, banjo, bones and tambourine, could dance a jig spiritedly if not excellently, and harbored the idea that he could compose songs. He had a mania for oratory and thought at first that he would be a tragedian but after prolonged consideration settled on minstrelsy as having the best opportunities -- a wise choice.

About this time, his parents moved again -- this time to Hartford, Connecticut, and in spite of school work, he found time to acquaint himself with the theatres and the managers of his new home town. He organized his first minstrel company here and played in that city and in the outlying villages. Of his myriad duties as the organizer and manager of this band of performers, he says:*

> "On the road I had been in the habit of going ahead of the company to the different towns, as agent, and returning at night to appear as principal end man and comedian, taking an active part in more than half of the performance. I contributed solos with the bones and tambourine, a burlesque stump speech, a big-shoe song and dance, the comedy character in the sketch A Ghost in a Pawnshop, and a part in the 'walk-around,' which was the finale, participated in by the entire company."

He thought so highly of this company that he was anxious to play in Boston itself, and did so in 1859, at Bumstead Hall on Tremont Street, where he played for two nights.

By 1860, although only seventeen years old, Leavitt had a wide working knowledge of management, and gathered an excellent troupe of variety and minstrel performers. With this company, he toured the New England states and the British provinces of north-eastern Canada. Chartering a sailing vessel in Boston, the troupe sailed for Yarmouth, Nova Scotia. The skipper had promised to make the trip in less than twenty-four hours but outside of the harbor, when just within sight of the village, the ship was becalmed and the company had to live for two days on salt pork and hardtack.

---

*ibid, p.73

With the first night's receipts from a full house at Ryerson's Hall in Yarmouth, Leavitt bought a used Concord coach and a team of horses, thus settling his transportation problem. The company consisted of twelve members, all versatile -- five for the orchestra, a small brass band for parades, a quartette and the necessary comedians, dancers and specialty performers -- all doubling, at least, if not tripling their duties.

There were no advertising or publicity costs. When entering a town, the band would strike up a lively tune -- the music being so unusual that the entire populace would flock about -- and that alone was enough to advertise the show for that night. Leavitt, as manager, paid all expenses, including the hotel bills which averaged daily from sixty to seventy-five cents per capita.

From Yarmouth, the company played the seaport towns en route to Halifax. From Shelburne, they took open boats to Cape Sable Isle but the reception accorded them was well worth the inconvenience. The islanders crowded the hall, each carrying a lighted lantern through the dense fog, presenting a novel sight. The troupe toured the provinces of Nova Scotia, New Brunswick, Prince Edward Island and Cape Breton. At Sydney, Cape Breton, where the inhabitants were mostly Scotch, Leavitt was greatly amused by overhearing a conversation in which one townsman said to another, referring to the show: "Angus, be ye goin' to th' desturrbance, th' nicht?"

BRANCHING OUT -- ON TOUR

In 1861 Leavitt organized the Leavitt's Sensation Combination Troupe which he sent to Cape Cod, Martha's Vineyard, Nantucket, and the manufacturing towns in the vicinity of Boston while his minstrels toured the larger cities and repeated the province tour. Leavitt believed that he was the first manager to own and operate more than one company at the same time.

About this time Leavitt was drafted for military service in the Union forces but complied with the **rules** for providing a substitute (for a consideration) through Thomas J. Gargan, recruiting officer who, after the war, became a well-known Boston politician and lawyer. Also, the second tour of the provinces being very remunerative, Leavitt had funds enough to make his initial venture in New York. Evidently it proved a failure, for the next week Leavitt was in Wilmington, Delaware, as manager and principal performer for John Weaver, the Yankee comedian, who was about to open Odd Fellows Hall there as a variety theatre. His weekly salary was fifteen dollars but since he could live in luxury at the Indian Queen Hotel for three dollars a week, the ratio of income and expense was not disproportionate. And then, too, during the Civil War, Wilmington was a convalescing station for disabled Union officers. Cash was plentiful and audiences often showed their appreciation of good performances by showering money upon the stage.

Annapolis, Maryland, was another city of the same type. Mart Lannan, proprietor of the National Hotel there, built a theatre and offered Leavitt the same job which he had been holding in Wilmington. Leavitt was here for several months, then left for Harrisburg, Pennsylvania, to direct the Theatre Comique, just opening there. The city was full of soldiers but business was sporadic, depending on the nature of war news. The Southern army was approaching uncomfortably near. One morning, the roar of cannons from the fields of Gettysburg, forty miles away, so alarmed the people of Harrisburg that great numbers of them fled. Box office receipts had so depreciated that the theatre was closed.

Leavitt returned to Wilmington and then rejoined the company at the Odd Fellows Hall for the rest of the season, during which time the troupe frequently played a night or two at the Old Coates Street Theatre in Philadelphia. At the termination of this engagement Leavitt returned to New York and joined Bishop and Florence's Minstrels for a short time. While the company was on a tour of the Atlantic states the two Harding Brothers, red-hot Southerners, got into a violent argument with some staunch Unionists in Wilkesbarre, Pennsylvania. A mob quickly formed, thinking that the whole company were Secessionists, and although the entertainment passed off quietly enough, an attack was made upon the performers in their dressing rooms after the show, and many of them, to escape assault, jumped out of the windows.

The Harding Brothers were immediately discharged,

but distorted and highly colored versions of the Wilkesbarre incident preceded the company and ruined their business for the rest of the tour. Following the premature finish of the Bishop and Florence Minstrels, Leavitt returned to New York and was engaged as manager and principal performer of the Olympic Minstrels, backed by wealthy men in Paterson, New Jersey. The company was good, but the receipts were not fabulous enough for the "angels" and they soon retired but the troupe continued for a time on a cooperative basis.

Having no show of his own on the road in the summer of 1863, Leavitt joined Richard Sand's Circus as a clown and blacked up for the side show in the minstrel scene after the regular performance. For several years he followed this occupation during the summer months although the work was hard and the salary small. The circuses at that time traveled by wagon and in order to save the livestock as much as possible from the heat of the day, the start was made very early in the morning. This cut down the sleeping time to two or three hours a day. Moreover, all hands were compelled to turn out and walk whenever a steep hill was encountered on their journey.

In 1864 he returned to Boston and assisted in the organization of Roberts and Wilson's Minstrels with such great names as Billy Emerson, Eph Horn, George Warren, James A. Barney, and Eugene Gorman answering the roll call of the cast. Leavitt was paired with Emerson as the end men. The company, though a great sensation, proved too expensive to be profitable. Salaries became irregular and pay days farther and farther apart till finally, in Lewiston, Maine, the big brass band instruments, which had been a feature of the show and belonged to the proprietors, were seized by the performers to satisfy their claims.

A SERIES OF ADVENTURES

Although only twenty-one, Leavitt was already more than a minstrel, a circus clown and a manager. Song writing was another of his achievements and he says:

> "...led to my composing 'Little Footsteps,' 'The Cot Where the Old Folks Died,' 'Darling Rosabel,' 'We Miss Thee from Our Cottage Home,' 'Yes, I Will Write Thee From Home' (answer to 'Write Me a Letter from Home'), 'The Little Grave Under the Willow,' 'Susie Brown,' 'At a Saturday Matinee,' 'The Mariner's Joy,' 'Our Little Humble Home,' 'Put My Little Shoes Away,' and other sentimental ballads, as well as comic ditties, published by Oliver Ditson, Boston, which were sung all over the country and were eagerly sought by leading minstrel artists.
>
> "I was also at this period turning out some pretty fair 'Poems,' which were readily accepted by the early magazines of Boston. In 1870, while in San Francisco, I disposed of upwards of twenty-five original lyrics to the leading music publishers, Sherman & Clay. In the early days of the civil conflict, I sang with my minstrel show, for the first time before the public, these war ballads, which became very popular: 'Dear Mother, I Have Come Home to Die,' 'Just Before the Battle, Mother,' also the songs, 'The Wearing of the Green,' 'Pat Malloy,' and the negro melodies, 'Young Eph's Lament,' 'Saucy Sam,' and 'The Union Cockade'."

The oil boom in Pennsylvania drew Leavitt next to that section of the country where he managed and played in hastily contrived "theatres" at Titusville, Pithole and Petroleum Centre. After a hectic time in the oil country, he returned to Boston and his minstrel career, re-engaging many of his former associates and some new ones. He took this company for a tour of the New England states.

The following season, in 1865, the Canadian provinces were covered by the company via Maine. After playing various cities, including three nights at Bangor, Maine, the company went to Oldtown, a thriving lumber shipping center. On the morning of the performance there, Leavitt had been to Bangor to order some printing, and when the train pulled into Vesey (about midway between the two points), he was astonished to find his entire company congregated on the station platform. They had walked from Oldtown to head him off, and declared that during the rehearsal a number of Indians, under the influence of alcoholic liquor, entered the hall and began to break up the musical instruments. Charles Laughton, the bass viol player (who later became Lieutenant Governor of Nevada), fought off the Indians with the aid of other members of the company until the police arrived.

The Oldtown scrimmage was so serious that the police had distributed revolvers to the members of the cast. Under these circumstances, the minstrels had tramped all the way to Vesey to warn Leavitt. He persuaded them to return to Oldtown and against the advice of the police and residents of the town they opened that night. The citizens, fearing another outbreak, remained away; consequently no entertainment was given.

From Oldtown, then, the company went to St. Andrews, New Brunswick, where, hearing that lobster fishing was very fine, the entire company went fishing and made a great catch. They requisitioned the hotel kitchen, had the lobsters boiled, and consumed them with quantities of milk. It was an extremely hot day, and the milk was nice and cool. That night, however, while in the dressing rooms blacking up for the evening, the entire company was afflicted with ptomaine poisoning. The local doctor, rushed hurriedly to the scene, came with a stomach pump and afforded relief to the agonized troupe. The curtain went up an hour and a half late but the audience, which had learned the cause of the delay, waited good naturedly. It was fully a week before the amateur fishermen were recovered.

A few days later at Fredericton, New Brunswick, Leavitt remained in the hotel to pay the bill after their performance in that town while the rest of the company waited for him on board the steamer en route to St. John where they were scheduled to appear the next night. Suddenly the hotel proprietor informed Leavitt that the last whistle had just sounded. Leavitt made for the wharf and found the boat at least five feet out. He made a running leap, diving through the wide open window of the cook's galley, much to the amazement of that functionary.

But this eventful trip was not yet over. After the provinces had been covered, the company headed down again to Maine. A steamer landed Leavitt at Eastport where they were to put on a two night entertainment and he found the papers headlined with the story of the assassination of President Lincoln. No sooner had the gangplank been lowered than an ominous cry was raised by the assembled townspeople. The Eastport citizens had noticed the resemblance of Leavitt to John Wilkes Booth and, the whereabouts of Booth being unknown as yet, had entertained serious doubts as to Leavitt's identity. The situation looked alarming as the crowd followed the company to the hotel but Leavitt went out on a verandah and made an explanation which seemingly was accepted, for no further disturbance occurred.

Early in the winter of 1867, Leavitt reorganized his minstrel company and leased Williams Hall, Boston, refitting it as a regular theatre. The opening was a great success. Leavitt, beside being the proprietor-manager, was also end man, playing the bones and cracking jokes. They had fine houses with good profits until the great snow of '67 which piled up to the windows of Williams Hall, twenty-five feet from the ground, and closed all the houses of entertainment in Boston.

The Boston reputation of the show made it ideal for the road, so the following spring and summer the company toured the larger cape towns as far as Provincetown, dropping in on the way at Nantucket and Martha's Vineyard. On this trip, one morning, while driving along the road skirting the ocean from Harwich to Provincetown, Leavitt saw his first whale, stranded on the beach.

EN ROUTE TO THE WEST

In 1868, after the close of a successful trip Leavitt made a visit to New York where he was induced by his friend R. M. Hooley, of Hooley's Minstrels, Brooklyn, New York, to join his company as substitute end man. During his second week, however, he accepted a position as manager and star of the Omaha Theatre Comique, nearing completion and shortly to be opened by Colonel Hanford. Omaha was a thriving railroad terminus and the theatre was packed nightly.

Leaving Omaha, he took his vaudeville company (among the earliest to cross the continent) westward, playing in such towns as Fremont, Julesburg, Cheyenne, Denver (by stage from Cheyenne to Denver) Laramie, Ogden, Salt Lake City, Elko, Reno, Virginia City, and all the other smaller towns on the railroad line between Omaha and San Francisco. They played in Corinne, Nevada, now a ghost city, in the days when it was a live, bustling town; and at Winnemucca, they played to an Indian audience, that town being the headquarters of the old Winnemucca tribe.

When this touring troupe of entertainers reached Sacramento, in 1869, Sheridan Corbyn, an agent of Thomas Maguire, the amusement magnate of the Pacific Coast, made a special trip from San Francisco to urge Leavitt to join Maguire's big minstrel company. Leavitt was hesitant about succeeding Joseph Murphy, who was a prime San Francisco favorite, but Corbyn was so insistent that Leavitt finally consented and ended his own tour. The members of his troupe immediately began engagements in the numerous variety halls of San Francisco.

Leavitt's salary was $175 a week -- and he earned it. He played the bones as end man, sang a number of original songs, recited a burlesque stump speech, performed an old man's specialty number, and appeared with Ben Cotton, the tambourine end man, in a negro act called The Rival Hotel Runners. Some of the employees in the Washington Market, San Francisco, had formerly worked in Faneuil Hall Market in Boston and, hearing that Leavitt was with the Maguire's Minstrels, turned out en masse to give their fellow townsman a rousing reception.

The minstrels played at the Washington Street Theatre but when The Black Crook was produced at this house, for the first time in California, the minstrels were forced to move to Mozart Hall. Maguire, during this period, was hard up for cash and salaries were not paid regularly. Therefore, when they received an offer to do two New Year's Day shows in Sacramento (1870), they gladly consented, returning again to Mozart Hall. Since the management again failed to pay him on time, Leavitt accepted an offer to be stage manager and headliner for a new variety theatre that was to be opened in

Virginia City, Nevada. He remained in Virginia City until the end of the season, then returning East.

VARIETY, BURLESQUE AND VAUDEVILLE

For almost a decade, throughout the seventies, Leavitt was building a reputation as one of the shrewdest managers in the business. He made yearly trips to Europe to engage the best Continental sensations; he toured America, signing up theatres all over the country to show his companies; he had dozens of troupes traveling over as many different routes, controlled from his New York office. In spite of these myriads of managerial duties, Leavitt was never on the short end of any business deal, whether in contracts with performers or with theatre managers. On the contrary, he considered all deals a moral defeat in which the profits were proportionately or fairly distributed.

Not only in the matter of legal papers and contracts was Leavitt so shrewd. He knew his public and knew it well; and public meant but one thing to him -- box-office receipts. When he, as a young man, decided against the legitimate stage, he turned to the lighter type of entertainment lock, stock and barrel. And during his ascendancy to his peak as a manager, the legitimate drama was on the decline. By this fortunate coincidence, Leavitt found his path beset with but few trifling obstacles -- and these served only to produce a salutary effect on his box-office.

In 1879, Leavitt brought a combination of Rentz's

Female Minstrels and Mabel Santley's English Burlesque Troupe -- a glorified leg-show -- to the Standard Theatre, San Francisco, on February 17. The San Francisco <u>Call</u> of February 18, 1879 described them as:

> "Hearty-looking girls, of the English type suggesting roast-beef and Yorkshire pudding with a 'drop of porter'; but their mental development appears to be in inverse ratio to their physical."

The performances of this forerunner of the "beef-trust" or what is known now as "girlesque" was, presumably, and naturally so, in direct ratio to their mental and physical development. Subtlety was thrown to the winds and their pieces were broad, bawdy and direct -- so much so that, according to the <u>Call</u> of March 15, M. B. Leavitt, manager and proprietor of the troupe, and ten girls of his company found themselves under arrest on the 14th of the month.

The trial was a newspaperman's holiday -- the city frowned publicly but avidly read the news account and followed the trial with suppressed snickers. Officer Miller, the arresting policeman, not only described but attempted to demonstrate the Can-Can, which he emphatically stated was "the most indecent he had ever witnessed." The City Physician, a widely-traveled man, stated that in all his experiences in Paris and Strasbourg, he had seen nothing as lewd as the Mabel Santley Can-Can. Prominent local citizens were witnesses, both for and against the defendants, and the jury received tickets to the show as Exhibit A. The special performance for the jury must have been memorable -- the verdict the next day was "Guilty."

During this period, Leavitt had from four to six vaudeville combinations each season on the road, apart from his many enterprises in other fields of amusement. They were known as Leavitt's Congress of European Celebrities, Leavitt's Gigantic Vaudeville Stars, M. B. Leavitt's All Star Specialty Company (the first time that the phrase 'All Star' had been used), M. B. Leavitt and Tony Pastor's United Combination (all principals engaged abroad) and others under various titles. The term "Vaudeville" in connection with a variety performance was used for the first time by Leavitt, he firmly believes, and although an incorrect use of the word, it has now supplanted the phrase "variety shows."

ESTABLISHED IN SAN FRANCISCO

The theatre in San Francisco was facing one of its darkest days with the decline of the California Theatre and the death of the legitimate drama. Leavitt had heard that several theatres were vacant in this formerly drama-conscious city and sent his agent to look over the field and select the best one to lease. His agent reported back that the condition of the San Francisco stage was deplorable and that it would be foolhardy to rent any theatre in the city. Leavitt was persistent, however, and came out to San Francisco himself for the specific purpose of checking on conditions.

In 1882 he took over the Bush Street Theatre, 325

Bush Street, formerly the Alhambra, and remained here for more than twenty years as lessee of the house, his name appearing for the first time in the city directory of 1889 as proprietor of the theatre.

Chroniclers of the period paid little or no attention to Leavitt's enterprises, evincing interest only in his business deals. The Argonaut of July 1, October 22, November 18 and December 2, 1882 carried brief mention of the progress of the business transaction. The Bush Street Theatre opened on the 23rd of December and the Argonaut of that day wrote:

> "...the man behind the scenes, who once invisibly pulled the strings is coming to the fore.... The managerial lithograph now faces you from the posting-walls, the centre of an elaborate medallion, with his combination grouped artistically about him, and his capitals in the bills, give him an individuality which he never possessed before.... The new man does not sing...songs, but he puts his capitals in the possessive and Leavitt's All-Star Specialty Troupe becomes a group of people without any particular individuality, singing under his direction. There is a familiar name here and there among them, notably Miss Flora Moore, whose clarion voice and songs a la Rooney are not forgotten...."

The review of the opening night, published in the Argonaut of December 30, was as cool and unimpressed:

> "...at the Bush Street Theatre, the Leavitt Specialty Company have brought little new with them, and of the new the St. Felix Sisters are the only striking feature.... Miss Flora Moore returns with her budget unchanged, but her mammoth note slightly lessened in volume. The others go to form the usual combinations of Irish, Dutch, and Negro specialists, with Mademoiselle Alphonsine, a globe revolver, and a

rather clever ventriloquist thrown in."

The performances seem not to have lived up to the grandiose promise of its advertising. The ad, which ran in the Morning Call, December 23, 1882 read as follows:

BUSH STREET THEATRE
M. B. Leavitt, Lessee and Manager
Al Hayman, Associate Manager

THE EVENT OF THE SEASON!

This (Saturday) Evening, December 23

Every evening(including Sunday)at 8. Wednesday and Saturday matinee at 2. Mr. M.B.Leavitt respectfully announces having secured an extended lease of this elegant theatre, and will, after thoroughly renovating the same, inaugurate his season with

LEAVITT'S ALL STAR SPECIALTY CO!

Specially reorganized, being the

GREATEST VAUDEVILLE ORGANIZATION
IN
AMERICA!

Kelly and Ryan, Lester and Allen, Flora Moore, 3-- St.Felix Sisters --3, Sinclair and Barnes, Fields and Hanson, Mlle.Alphonsine, Annie Boyd, Harry Morris, Chalet, and the Four Diamonds -- Wilson, Sawtelle, Brevarde and Gilmore.

SPECIAL MATINEES
Christmas and New Year's Day at 2

Prices of Admission
Reserved Seats,Orchestra and Dress Circle $1.50
Orchestra and Dress Circle................ $1.00
Family Circle............................. $0.50
Matinees......................75¢, 50¢ and 25¢

Items which interested the newspapers in connection with Leavitt were those such as the following which appeared in the Morning Call, December 31, 1882:

> "M. B. Leavitt is said to have lent $12,000 to the Metropolitan Job Office as some return for the 'points' Henry, of the Herald, gave him by which Mike is said to have cleared $50,000 in Manhattan stock."

The San Francisco newspapers continued to be unexcited about Leavitt's productions. They were dull, no doubt, after the furore caused by the arrest of his Mabel Santley troupe of dancers. And Leavitt no longer appeared on the stage. He was busy with his several road shows, directing their itinerary, drawing up contracts, and often acting as advance agent when breaking into a virgin territory.

SUCCESS AND AFFLUENCE

His trip through Mexico, for instance, was successful in more ways than one. The Argonaut, November 26, 1887 in their first mention of him in their pages for that year, reported:

> "M. B. Leavitt, the lessee of the Bush Street Theatre, has had a lucky windfall. Some months ago he inaugurated a theatrical circuit in the South, which included the City of Mexico, and, during a visit there last year, made the acquaintance of an eccentric old bachelor, Don Pedro Quintes. They became fast friends, and the Don dying a few days ago, left Leavitt a fortune of two hundred thousand dollars."

Other newspaper comments were hardly favorable in tone. The same periodical of October 16, 1886 wrote:

> "The Bush Street Theatre is to be closed next week for necessary repairs. The dressing-room accommodations are to be enlarged. The sewerage is also to be attended to -- a very

important improvement."

And again on June 18, 1887:

> "The Bush Street Theatre actually rejoices in a new piece of scenery."

In contradiction of Leavitt's own estimate of his importance in the theatrical history of California, as stated in his book, Fifty Years in Theatrical Management:

> "...and when the history of the Golden State is finally written, I am content in the belief that my share of its theatrical life must ever remain one of its most important chapters; and in saying this, I do not believe that I am too far jeopardizing modesty,"

The Morning Call, May 6, 1888 in an article headed "The Value of Word in Season," said:

> "Mr. M. B. Leavitt once got heartening advice from his manager, Charlie Hall, that was worth a great deal of money to him in his connection with the Bush Street (Theatre). It was after the failure of the Wyndham Comedy Company, some five years ago, and when M. B. felt very blue and oppressed with doubt as to the future of the Bush. He wanted to give up the ship and strike his flag. If we do not mistake Hayman was allied with him at that time in the management -- he went below at once.
>
> "But Hall advised Leavitt to hold on and take a reef in his lower lip, that sagged much indeed. 'Do you think it's worth while going on?' he asked Hall. 'Certainly; we haven't secured the right kind of a show for the house this season, but look out well for the next.'
>
> "The value of Hall's words is in this: that since they were uttered the Bush Street (Theatre) has made for Leavitt $180,000 by 'striking the right kind of show.' He offered $150,000 for the property a few years ago but the owner concluded he would rather keep him as a tenant...."

In 1888, the California Theatre was razed by the

owners. Before this occurred, however, Leavitt decided to capitalize on the nostalgic fame of the old house and leased it for its last four weeks. His favorite Rentz-Santley Minstrels were to occupy the stage during the month of July -- minstrels, comedians, leg-show artists, the whole company,

> "...high-kickers and all (reported the Morning Call, June 24) -- a last kick, which the old house might have been spared."

On the first of July the same paper, in an article titled "The Leg-itimate vs. The Legitimate," said:

> The last month of all that ends the 'strange, eventful history' of the California Theatre begins tomorrow with M. B. Leavitt's celebrated Rentz-Santley Novelty and Burlesque Company."

At the close of the holiday season of 1888-1889, Leavitt's business at the Bush Street Theatre had so increased that he closed the theatre for three weeks for alterations. It reopened on January 26, 1889 with the Lydia Thompson English Burlesque Company. The San Francisco Chronicle, (which was friendlier to Leavitt than any of the other local papers -- no doubt due to the theatrical and business connections of M. H. de Young, owner and publisher) of January 27, reported:

> "The new Bush Street Theatre opened its doors to the public for the first time last night, and the public were there in such numbers that long before the curtain went up they were turned away in crowds. Mr. Leavitt has made a success of his theatre...."

The article continued with much praise for the architectural changes in the theatre but it was forced to admit that the play was a failure. The English company was well-trained but the performances did not please the Americans. It was not their kind of burlesque.

The <u>Morning Call</u> also devoted columns of space to the $20,000 alterations in the building in the issues of January 6, 13, 20, 25 and 27, 1889 but had little to say of the performances. On February 26, however, the paper gave much space to another adventure that Leavitt had with the police:

> "M. B. Leavitt, lessee of the Bush Street Theatre, was arrested yesterday by Officer Harry Hook on a charge of obstructing the aisles of the theatre. Last Saturday evening there was not seating room for the audience, and as on similar occasions camp stools were placed in the aisles, contrary to the fire ordinance. Mr. Leavitt was reminded at the time that it was not legal, but he paid no attention to the police officer's notice. A warrant was therefore sworn out for his arrest."

This was good publicity for his theatre as he could not have bought better advertising of the fact that he had packed houses.

For a few years the Bush Street Theatre's business boomed, Leavitt booking varied entertainments here from comic opera to animal acts. Late in the 1890's, the popularity of the house waned and it was closed. One house more or less did not make an appreciable dent in Leavitt's pocketbook, for he was now the central booking agent for dozens of houses and hundreds of performers throughout the country. But in August of 1898 he decided to reopen the long-closed Bush

Street Theatre under a new name -- the Comedy Theatre.

For his first production he offered more than mere theatrical amusement. Mrs. Romualdo Pacheco, wife of the ex-Governor of California, had written several plays which had enjoyed great success in New York. Leavitt induced her to put on the premiere of her latest play, The Leading Man, at the opening of the new theatre. This fortunate combination received much publicity and public interest.

The San Francisco Chronicle of August 26 gave Mrs. Pacheco a long story, mentioning that

> "Ex-Governor Pacheco, who has been spending a few weeks at Lake Tahoe...accompanied his wife to San Francisco."

And on the following day, the Chronicle reported:

> "Mrs. Romualdo Pacheco, a lady who has achieved a marked degree of success in plays composed by her, arrived in town Thursday and has taken apartments at the Occidental. Mrs. Pacheco needs no introduction to the people of California, for her home has been here for many years, and she is well known for her strong intellectuality and gracious manner. She has come here to supervise the production of her latest play, The Leading Man, which will serve to open the... Comedy on Friday, September 2."

The advertisement which ran in the Chronicle on August 28, read:

NEW COMEDY THEATRE
(Formerly the Popular Bush)

Direction, M. B. Leavitt.......Alf Ellinghouse,
Resident Mgr.

THE SOCIETY EVENT

Grand Opening...Sept. 2

$10,000 -- Involving an Expenditure of -- $10,000
....
POPULAR PRICES

```
Entire Orchestra.............................75¢
Dress Circle.................................50¢
Box Seats................................. $1.00
Balcony..............................50¢ and 35¢
Gallery..............................25¢ and 15¢
```

Reviews of the opening night of the Comedy Theatre which appeared in both the Call and the Chronicle echoed each other in calling the house "bright," "attractive" and "handsome." On the merit of the play, both were rather non-committal. The Call, September 3, 1898:

"New Comedy Theatre Opens
A Crowded House Greets
'The Leading Man'

The Remodeled Theatre
Is Very Pretty

"The new Comedy Theatre, bright and handsome as a new Easter bonnet, opened its doors to the public last night under conditions that made glad the hearts of Managers Leavitt and Ellinghouse and thoroughly pleased a fashionable and critical audience. The alterations and improvements are so complete that the old time patrons of the former Bush Street Theatre could hardly realize it. Everything is up-to-date, uniformed ushers, cozy retiring rooms for ladies and gentlemen and all things in the way of comforts that could be expected...."

The San Francisco Chronicle, August 28:

"The Bush Street Theatre, transformed into a bright and attractive house of amusement, refurnished and decorated tastefully...as the new Comedy Theatre...quite a fashionable event...."

and again on September 3:

"The old Bush Street Theatre became the new

> Comedy last night, and it looked as bright and gay as if it were the days when it was one of the most popular houses...."

and finally on September 11:

> "...special attention should be drawn to the new curtain of the new Comedy Theatre. It is one of the most artistic things in the city, a scene from As You Like It, admirably painted by the well-known artist, Charles D. Robinson...."*

For several more years Leavitt remained the lessee of this house in San Francisco, making frequent trips to this city to remain in constant personal touch with the performances in the Comedy Theatre.

RETIRES FROM SAN FRANCISCO AFTER 20 YEARS

With the Great Fire of 1906, which temporarily disrupted all theatrical business in San Francisco, Leavitt gave up all business connections in this city and fled to a comparative security in New York, never returning to California again. He retired from all active participation in theatres in 1908 to devote his time to the writing of his memoirs, Fifty Years in Theatrical Management, which appeared in 1912.

In 1919, Leavitt moved to Miami Beach, Florida to establish his home where the climate would be more salubrious, for he was then seventy-six years old and the years of intense work without vacations had drained his vitality. This was a wise choice -- or perhaps the veteran showman had too

---

*Son of Dr. D. G. "Yankee" Robinson, theatrical pioneer in San Francisco.

tenacious a hold on life to let mere years take their toll -- for he celebrated his ninety-second birthday on June 25, 1935, in spite of a bad fall that he had suffered a few days previously.

But injuries received in this accident were more severe than first suspected. Immediately after his simple birthday celebration -- spent very quietly -- he became exceedingly weak and fell into a coma. Two days later, June 27, 1935 he died. He was a charter member of the Benevolent Protective Order of Elks, having been one of the original thirteen who founded the organization and, as the oldest Elk in years of membership, was an honorary life member. He was survived by his widow, Lida Elizabeth Leavitt.

And so the man who said "I will not admit that any one else has had more to do with the amusement business in the land of gold than myself. No other had more extensive operations than I...."* found himself with a good-sized fortune but no acclaim or recognition from chroniclers of the time.

Leavitt, however, was more than an astute business man limited to the confines of his own enterprises. He saw clearly the evils of the contemporary Klaw and Erlanger monopoly on the stage and fought bitterly against it. In his memoirs, he writes:

---

*Fifty Years of Theatrical Management p. 241

"It may be true, as some sapient writers on stage topics contempuously assert, that the public cares to hear nothing about the business side of the theatre -- that all it really wants to know is what the show is, who appears in it, and have these bald facts illumined with large quantities of tittle-tattle about the personalities and private affairs of actors and actresses. The general dumbness of the press on the conduct of so important a commercial industry as that of the theatre goes to bear out the assertion, and would confirm it if it were not generally understood that theatrical managers who were extensive advertisers for the past few years preferred to have the courtesy of silence extended to their methods.

"There is no doubt, though, that it is a matter of importance to the public how that business is conducted. In the modern scheme of things no art is so much influenced by its commercial side as that of the stage. But dramatic art has become complex in its representation; author and artist are dependent on shrewd management. The barn and the tent no longer give opportunity to the budding genius. Dramatic art is dependent upon the business of the theatre and the way it is conducted."

Believing thoroughly in this, it was natural for him to do everything in his power to crush the powerful syndicate and the censorship by the press, its ally. That he had a personal ax to grind as the competitor of the syndicate became negligible in the light of this broader issue. "The manager and his ways are as legitimate subjects of criticism and discussion as the art and its interpreters," he wrote.

Thus, for twenty years, California and San Francisco particularly, had in charge of its lighter entertainments the man who conceived the present form of vaudeville, the vaudeville circuit, booking agency, and the four-in-one performer-manager-agent-theatre contracts. Most noteworthy -- or at least the one longest remembered -- of his contributions to the American stage is the present form of the burlesques. The leg-shows have become an American institution, following an almost classical rigidity of form, and it was Leavitt who introduced it to San Francisco.

The notorious Barbary Coast of San Francisco -- running wide open, with its burly, bawdy night life, from the discovery of gold to the enactment of prohibition -- owes much to the female minstrels, the sexy dances and the abbreviated costumes imported by Leavitt which gave Pacific Street its world fame. Both sides of the symbolical railroad tracks, from up-town to down-town San Francisco, in the twenty years from 1882 to 1906 that Leavitt remained here, owed much to him in the way of frothy entertainment. San Francisco today owes him much for the atmosphere and the color that it has as an amusement center of America.

M. B. LEAVITT

SOME OF HIS BUSINESS ASSOCIATES

Leavitt had the fortunate faculty of picking the right men to aid him in his business enterprises. Several of them rose to important positions in their profession. In the year 1912 when Leavitt had retired from active participation in the theatrical business, his former associates had become leading lights in the field of the theatre. Some of the most prominent ones and their position in 1912 were:

Al Hayman, president of the "Theatrical Syndicate"
Martin Beck, head of the "Great Orpheum Circuit"
George W. Lederer, musical comedy producer
Frederick F. Proctor, vaudeville magnate, former partner of
    B. F. Keith
David Warfield, noted actor.
George H. Broadhurst, noted dramatist
Edgar Smith, author of travesties and musical comedies
Sidney Rosenfeld, another leading dramatist
Gustav Luders, prolific musical composer
Marcus R. Mayer, manager of American and European stars
William Morris, independent vaudeville magnate
Jacob J. Gottlob, chief of Pacific Coast managers
Henry S. Sanderson, partner of F. F. Proctor
Charles P. Hall, in control of important outlying California
    theatres
Kit Clarke, made a fortune in jewelry trade, retired
John E. Warner, assistant secretary, Nat'l Ass'n of producing
    Mgrs.
Hollis E. Cooley, general manager for Felix Isman
George Dance, English theatrical magnate, author and producer
James J. Armstrong, past exalted ruler, N. Y. Lodge, No. 1,
    B.P.O.E.
Jay Rial, executive head of Ringling Bros. press department
John P. Hill, secretary of the "White Rats" Association
Walter J. Kingsley, general press representative

BOOKING MANAGERS WHO WORKED FOR LEAVITT

Dudley McAdow, associate of Stair and Havlin
Ed. V. Giroux, gen'l manager of John Cort's enterprises
James H. Curtin, representative for Empire Burlesque Circuit
J. J. Rosenthal, representative for Al. H. Woods' enterprises
James H. Decker, booking manager for the Shuberts
Harry A. Lee, booking manager for Klaw and Erlanger

PERFORMERS AND COMPANIES UNDER LEAVITT'S MANAGEMENT

Minnie Maddern (Fiske)
Wyndham Comedy Co.
Neil Burgess & Co.
Emerson's Minstrels
Charley Reed
Billy Sweatman
Sol Smith Russell & Co.
Lily Post
Katherine Krieg
John L. Sullivan Big Vaudeville
   and Athletic Combination
Janet Waldorf & Co.
Bobby Gaylor
European Specialty & Novelty Co.
Spanish Opera Co.
Romualdo Pacheco's Ideal Comedy
   Co.
Reilly & Woods
Sadie Martinot
Moore & Burgess Minstrels
Violet Cameron
Leavitt's English Folly &
   Burlesque Co:
   W. W. Walton
   Frank Wright
   Cyrus & Maude
   M. Kloss & Mlle. Kloss
   Emily Lyndale
   Mlle. Price
   Mlle. Cora Anita Phillips
   Ruby Stuart
   Chester Sisters
   Connie Leslie
   Ella Dean
   Beatrice Vaughn
Leavitt's All Star Specialty
   Company:
   Flora Moore
   St. Felix Sisters
   Mlle. Alphonsine
Mlle. Aimee
Ben Cotton's Co.
Daly's Company:
   Ada Rehan
   Edith Kingdon
   M. B. Curtis
   John Drew
   Otis Skinner
   James Lewis
   William Gilbert

W. T. Carleton Light Opera
   Co.
Rosina Vokes London Comedy
   Co.
Washington Irving Bishop
Daniel H. Harkins
Frank Mordaunt
Theodore Hamilton
Rowland Buckstone
Amelia Bingham
Alice Harrison
Viola Clifton
William Lester
Paul Allen
Bobby Newcomb
The Great Ellwood
Lew Spencer
Harry Armstrong
The Triple Alliance:
   Imro Fox
   Leroy
   Powell
Emma Carus
Nate Salsbury
Mme. d'Escozas
Cuenca
Professor Carpenter
Harry Kellar
"The Clemenceau Case" Co:
   Sybil Johnson
Rose Coghlan
Verona Jarbeau
William Elton
Louis Massen
W. J. Montgomery
B. T. Ringgold
W. L. Branscombe
Minna Phillips
Sarah Maddern
Ed. Lay
Lee & Zancig
   Sylvian A. Lee
   Mr. & Mrs. Julius Zancig
Louise Willis Hepner
Mme. Pilar Morin
Leonora White
De Villiers
Theodore Jackson
Joe Murphy
Maggie Mitchell

PERFORMERS AND COMPANIES UNDER LEAVITT'S MANAGEMENT (Cont.)

Mrs. William J. Florence
Margaret Mather
John T. Raymond
Wilson Barrett
Henri de Vries
Lydia Thompson English
   Burlesque Co.
Rentz-Santley Minstrel Co:
   Mabel Santley
   Hattie Forrest
   Rosa Lee
   Kate Raynham
   Ada Werner
   Della Zittella
   Flora Plimsoli
   Nellie McDermott
   Kate McDermott
   Lulu Mortimer
Nightingale Serenaders
Leavitt's Gigantean Minstrel Co.
Johnny Allen
McIntyre & Heath
Kelly & Ryan
Lester & Allen
Leavitt's Sensation Combination
   Troupe
Louise Montague
W. F. (Buffalo Bill) Cody
George Frothingham
Levantine Brothers:
   F. F. Proctor
John T. Kelly:
   Kelly & Ryan
   Kelly & Mason
Charles Laughton
E. M. Hall
Kate Pennoyer
Madame Garetta
Hyers Sisters' Musical
   Organization
Lew Benedict
Nellie Sylvester
Jennie Melville
   Melville & Stetson
Leavitt's Congress of European
   Celebrities
Leavitt's Gigantic Vaudeville
   Stars
M. B. Leavitt & Tony Pastor
   United Combination

Samuel J. Ryan
Col. Ira A. Paine
Harrigan & Hart
   Tony Hart
   Edward Harrigan
Liza Weber
Phyllis Glover
Louise Balfe
Cyril Maude
Bartholomew's Equine
   Paradox
Pauline Markham
Frank Lawler
Sallie Swift
Willie Edouin American
   Musical Comedy Co.
Marie de Lecour
Mlle. Sara (Wiry Sal)
Winetta Montague
Sara Nelson
Georgie Leigh
Marie Pascoe
Florie Plimsoll
McKee Rankin's Co.
Madame Dolaro
Vienna Ladies' Orchestra
Hyers Sisters, Mada & Louise
Dan Emmett
Dave Reed
Archie Hughes
Sam Sanford
Frank Moran
Cool Burgess
Marie Williams
Lizzie Mulholland
Fanny Wentworth
Adelaide Praeger
Minnie Marshall
Daisy Ramsden
Camille D' Elmar
Alma Stuart Stanley
Laura Trevor
Matt Robson
James A. Meade
J. W. Bradbury
Louis Kellaher
Frank Hinde
Lewis Fink
Signor Novissimo
Frank Musgrave

PERFORMERS AND COMPANIES UNDER LEAVITT'S MANAGEMENT (Cont.)

Monte Cristo Burlesque Co.	Julia St. Clair
Annie Dunscombe	Sadie Martinot
Clara Mabel	"City Directory" Co:
Lillie Furneau	Willie Collier
Prof. Alexander Herrmann	Charley Reed
Alice Atherton	James T. Powers
Richard Golden	"Electric Doll" Co:
Dora Wiley	Frank Daniels
Atkinson's Jollities	Jennie Yeamans
Signor Operti	Nellie Bouverie
Louise Davis	

THEATRES MANAGED OR LEASED BY LEAVITT

Odd Fellows Hall	Wilmington, Del.	Manager
National Theatre	Annapolis, Md.	Manager
Theatre Comique	Harrisburg, Pa.	Director
Orpheum Theatre	San Francisco	Booking Agent
Bush St. Theatre	San Francisco	Lessee, Manager
Theatre Comique	Omaha, Neb.	Stage Manager
Academy of Music	Denver, Colo.	Booking Agent
Tabor Grand	Denver	Booking Agent
Robinson Hall	New York	Lessee
Terrace Garden	New York	Lessee
Halsted St. Opera House	Chicago	Lessee
Burlington Hall	Chicago	Lessee
Globe Theatre	New Orleans	Lessee
Metropolitan Theatre	New York	Lessee
Williams Hall	Boston	Manager, Lessee
Windsor Theatre	Chicago	Manager, Lessee
Grand Opera House	San Francisco	Booking Agent
Baldwin Theatre	San Francisco	Booking Agent
Standard Theatre	San Francisco	Manager, Lessee
Royal Avenue Theatre	London	Lessee
Hooley's Theatre	Chicago	Booking Agent
Olympic Theatre	New York	Lessee
Tony Pastor's Theatre	New York	Lessee
Boston Theatre	Boston	Booking Agent
St. James Hall	Buffalo, N. Y.	Booking Agent
Court Theatre	Liverpool	Booking Agent
Third Avenue Theatre	New York	Lessee
Broadway Theatre	Denver	Booking Agent
Comedy Theatre	New York	Booking Agent
Marquam Grand Opera	Portland, Ore.	Lessee

PRESS AGENTS WHO WORKED FOR LEAVITT

Ed. A. Abrams
Jas. J. Armstrong
Charles Benton
Matt L. Berry
William Black
C. Armory Bruce
Thomas X. Burnside
W. J. Chapelle
Charles Chase
Max Clayton
W. S. Cleveland
Chas. H. Day
J. H. Decker
Claude de Haven
William Eversole
Wolf Falk
William Foote
Ed. V. Giroux
E. M. Gotthold
George Gouge
Charles B. Griste
Harry B. Hapgood
Chas. Harkenson
E. P. Hilton
D. B. Hodges
John Hooley
Dan B. Hopkins
J. M. Hyde
Chas. H. Keeshin
Bruno Kenincott
George H. Knapp
J. H. Lane
Abe Leavitt
Harry A. Lee
Matt Leland
H. B. Lonsdale
E. B. Ludlow
H. E. Manchester
Joseph Chenet

William Mandeback
Joel Marks
Frank W. Martineau
Dudley McAdow
Charles McGeachy
Andy McKay
Charles Melville
George Millbank
Arthur Miller
J. W. Morrissey
Josh E. Ogden
H. E. Parmelee
Augustus Pennoyer
David Peyser
Harry Phillips
Jay Rial
Chas. W. Roberts
N. D. Roberts
Emil Rosenbaum
J. J. Rosenthal
Harry W. Seamon
Harry Seymour
W. H. Sherman
Charles Slocum
Harry C. Smart
Abe Spitz
George W. Stanhope
Edw. S. Stanley
Ernest Stanley
Henry M. Stanley
W. H. Strickland
Geo. S. Sidney
Mark Thall
Sam Thall
Edward Thurnaer
E. B. Vosberg
Marshall P. Wild
Arthur Williams
Charles A. Wing
Ben Wyckoff

M. B. LEAVITT

BIBLIOGRAPHY

Hart, Jerome A.   In Our Second Century (The Pioneer Press, San Francisco, 1931) pp. 410, 426

Leavitt, M. B.   Fifty Years in Theatrical Management (Broadway Publishing Co., New York, 1912)

Madison, James   San Francisco Century of Commerce Celebration (1835-1935) article by Madison, James on Early San Francisco Theatres, p. 29, (A Historical programme in the clippings file of the Music Department of the San Francisco Public Library)

NEWSPAPERS AND PERIODICALS

Argonaut   (San Francisco), Jan. 7, 1880; July 1, Oct. 28, Nov. 18, Dec. 2, 23, 30, 1882; April 7, June 2, 30, Aug. 4, 1883; Jan. 3, July 14, 18, Aug. 15, 22, Sept. 26, 1885; Oct. 16, 1886; Feb. 19, June 18, Oct. 29, Nov. 26, 1887; Dec. 24, 1888; Jan. 7, 21, 1889.

Morning Call   (San Francisco), Mar. 15, 27, Apr. 4, 12, 13, Dec. 23, 31, 1882; Jan. 1, 5, 22, Apr. 29, May 6, 20, June 17, 24, July 1, 15, Aug. 5, Sept. 23, 30, Nov. 4, Dec. 2, 16, 23, 28, 1888; Jan. 6, 13, 20, 25, 27, Feb. 26, 1889; Aug. 27, Sept. 3, Nov. 20, 27, 1898.

The Chronicle   (San Francisco), Dec. 16, 1888; January 27, Mar. 3, 10, 1889; Jan. 29, Feb. 5, 6, 12, 1890; Aug. 4, 21, 26, 27, 28, Sept. 3, 11, 1898.

Daily Critic   (San Francisco), Feb. 13, March 28, May 20, 1868.

Examiner   (San Francisco), March 12, 1899.

New York Times   (New York), June 28, 1935.

PROJECT EDITORIAL STAFF

Research Director.....Jack W. Wilson

MONOGRAPH WRITERS

George Ducasse   Alan Harrison
Cornel Lengyel   Eddie Shimano

RESEARCH ASSISTANTS

Mathew Gately   Gretchen Clark
Dorothy Phillips   Lenore Legere
Lauretta Bauss   Florence Bradley
       Wyland Stanley

ART and PHOTO REPRODUCTION

Lala Eve Rivol   M. H. Mc Carty

PRODUCTION

William K. Noe   Elleanore Staschen
       Clara Mohr

Although the entire research and stenographic staff on the project assisted in the preparation of these monographs at various stages in production, particular credit should be given to Mr. Cornel Lengyel for his work on the Maguire monograph, and to Mr. Eddie Shimano for his work on the Robinson and Leavitt monographs.

                       Lawrence Estavan
                       Project Supervisor.

www.ingramcontent.com/pod-product-compliance
Lightning Source LLC
Chambersburg PA
CBHW080441110426
42743CB00016B/3240